Zelda Marsh

Copyright

Copyright © 2025 Zelda Marsh

All rights reserved. No part of this publication may be reproduced, distributed, or transmitted in any form or by any means, including photocopying, recording, or other electronic or mechanical methods, without the prior written permission of the author, except in the case of brief quotations embodied in critical reviews and specific other non-commercial uses permitted by copyright law.

First Edition

This is a work of nonfiction. To protect their privacy, some individuals' names and identifying details have been changed.

The information in this book is based on the author's personal experiences and is not intended to replace professional medical or psychological advice. Always consult qualified healthcare providers for medical and mental health concerns.

Published by Zelda Marsh, Queensland, Australia

Cover design by Zelda Marsh

ISBN: 9798281606943

Dedication

For my little brother, Croy, who didn't make it. I couldn't save you then, darling, but these words might save someone else now. The healing I found wasn't what either of us expected – a quiet strength discovered in the deepest shadows, but it's no less real for that. Your memory lives in every page of this book and every day of my life. May your spirit find peace, and may your story, through mine, offer a flicker of hope to others.

Zelda Marsh

Note to Reader

Dear Reader,

If you're holding this book, I already see you, darling. Whether you're deep in the ache or starting to crack open the idea of healing like a stubborn Cleethorpes cockle, I need you to know this: you're not broken, and you're not alone, though God knows it feels like it sometimes.

I didn't write this to impress anyone. Not bloody likely! I wrote it because I was done waiting for closure that never came, forgiveness that was never offered, and permission that no one would ever give me. About as useful as waiting for the tide to go out at Cleethorpes when you're already soaked to the bone.

My truth is raw, messy, painful, and sometimes painfully funny because humour saved me when nothing else could, like finding a chip shop open at midnight when you're starving.

There's no gold medal at the end of trauma, no parade down Freeman Street. But there is freedom. And it starts when you stop living in someone else's version of your story. Their version's about as useful as a chocolate teapot, anyway.

www.manifestmerriment.com

I Don't Need Your Forgiveness To Heal

Note To Reader

Dear Reader,

If you're holding this book, I already see you, darling. Whether you're deep in the ache or starting to crack open the idea of healing like a stubborn Cleethorpes cockle, I need you to know this: you're not broken, and you're not alone, though God knows it feels like it sometimes.

I didn't write this to impress anyone. Not bloody likely! I wrote it because I was done waiting for closure that never came, forgiveness that was never offered, and permission that no one would ever give me. About as useful as waiting for the tide to go out at Cleethorpes when you're already soaked to the bone.

My truth is raw, messy, painful, and sometimes painfully funny because humour saved me when nothing else could, like finding a chip shop open at midnight when you're starving.

There's no gold medal at the end of trauma, no parade down Freeman Street. But there is freedom. And it starts when you stop living in someone else's version of your story. Their version's about as useful as a chocolate teapot, anyway.

This book is your permission slip to take up space, feel the stuff you've been told to hide, let your body say what your mouth never could, and come home to yourself. Like finally

Zelda Marsh

getting back to your own bed after a night of God-awful karaoke and too many pints.

Read it like a hug. Or a slap. Or a proper natter over a brew with your wisest, sweariest mate who doesn't sugar-coat a bloody thing but loves you anyway.

Whatever it is... Let it be yours. Because darling, you've earned that much.

With all my truth and then some.

Zelda Marsh

I Don't Need Your Forgiveness To Heal

Introduction

Some books change your life because they're so profound, beautifully written, and intellectually stimulating that they shift your worldview.

This isn't one of those books.

This book might change your life, but not because it's pretty, polished, or perfect. It might change your life because it's real. It says the things we're not supposed to say. It challenges the toxic positivity and spiritual bypassing that's become the wallpaper of the wellness industry.

And because, quite frankly, it might make you laugh until you snort tea out your nose, which, as it turns out, is surprisingly therapeutic.

This book is about trauma. Not the sanitised, Instagram-friendly version where everything ends with a neat bow and a motivational quote. The real version. The messy, complicated, sometimes darkly funny version that lives in your body long after your mind has tried to move on.

It's about how trauma shapes us physically, emotionally, neurologically, how it creates patterns we don't even recognise until we're repeating them for the hundredth time, how it lives in our nervous systems, relationships, and daily choices.

But mostly, it's about healing. It is not the kind that comes from forgiveness, though it is brilliant if that works for you. It is the kind that comes from reclamation, from boundaries. Finally, finally, putting yourself first after a lifetime of being last. And yes, from finding absurd humour in even the darkest moments.

I didn't write this book because I'm healed. I wrote it because I'm healing. Because I'm still figuring it out. Because I've learned some things the hard way, that might make your journey a little easier. And because sometimes, when everything is falling apart, the only thing left to do is laugh.

That's not flippant, by the way. Humour has been my lifeline. My Northern Lincolnshire wit has saved me more times than I can count. When I was a kid with twisted legs, a teenager living off stolen HP sauce, or an adult navigating a relationship that mirrored my earliest wounds, laughter was often the only thing that kept me going.

Science backs this up, by the way. Laughter releases endorphins, reduces stress hormones, and activates the parasympathetic nervous system—the exact opposite of what trauma does to our bodies. It's not just comic relief; it's physiological medicine.

But beyond the science, humour does something even more powerful: it gives us perspective. It allows us to step back from our pain just enough to see that we are not our trauma. Even in our darkest moments, some of us can still find the absurdity, irony, and unexpected punchline in our own story.

Humour breaks through denial, too. It lets us tell the truth when it is too painful to face head-on. It's why I can write about stealing condiments as a homeless teenager or about my body's dramatic betrayals with a wry smile rather than crushing despair. It's not about minimising the pain—it's about making it bearable enough, actually, to look at it.

This book isn't a step-by-step guide. It's not "**Trauma Healing for Dummies.**" It's a conversation, a story, a hand reaching out in the dark to say, "*I've been here too. You're not alone. And yes, we can laugh about this someday, maybe even today.*"

It's divided into three parts:

Part One: The Wounds explores the origins of trauma, how it imprints on the developing brain and body, shapes our earliest understanding of ourselves and the world, and creates patterns that can last a lifetime if left unaddressed. And yes, sometimes, the most painful stories have moments of unexpected comedy.

Part Two: The Body Keeps Score delves into the physical manifestations of trauma, how it lives in our tissues, nervous systems, unconscious, and responses. How does the body explain to members what the mind tries to forget? And how sometimes we express what we can't say in ways that are both painful and, in retrospect, darkly comical.

Part Three: Reclamation & Healing offers a path forward, not a perfect, linear path, but a messy, human one. It explores how we can reclaim our power, set boundaries, create safety, and find freedom without waiting for anyone else's permission or forgiveness. It also celebrates the healing power of inappropriate laughter, of finding humour in the absurdity of it all.

Throughout my story, I weave research, science, and practical tools. Humour is found in dark places because sometimes laughter is the only way through. Reflection prompts invite you to explore your own experience at your own pace.

This book won't fix you because you're not broken. It won't heal you because that's your journey, not mine. But it might offer some company along the way. Some validation. Some hope. Some permission to be exactly where you are, feeling exactly what you think. And maybe, a few moments where you laugh out loud despite yourself.

And perhaps most importantly, it will help you see that your healing has never depended on anyone else. It's always been yours to claim. And sometimes, the most revolutionary act is to find something to laugh about when the world expects you to cry.

So, let's begin with honesty, compassion, evidence-based approaches, and our sense of humour firmly intact. Because if there's one thing I've learned, healing doesn't have to be solemn to be sacred.

Table of Contents

DETAILED TABLE OF CONTENTS

PART ONE: THE WOUNDS

Where trauma begins and how it shapes us

Chapter 1: Born Into Brokenness
- The physical challenges of my early years
- Childhood sexual trauma and the body's first betrayal
- When those meant to protect you don't
- How early experiences wire the developing brain
- The Northern English way of coping: humour as survival

Chapter 2: Abandonment & Its Aftermath
- When mother leaves: the eight-year-old caretaker
- The body's response to emotional abandonment
- Father's emotional unavailability and its lasting impact
- Hypervigilance as a childhood survival strategy
- The foundations of people-pleasing and perfectionism

Chapter 3: Teenage Turmoil
- Running away at fourteen and living on stolen condiments

- The body under stress: survival mode in adolescence
- Reproductive trauma at seventeen
- How teenage experiences shape identity formation
- Finding humour in the darkest places

Chapter 4: Ancestral Patterns: The Inherited Trauma

- The science of epigenetics: how trauma alters gene expression
- The "Family Tree of Dysfunction" and repeating patterns
- Northern English cultural context and generational silence
- How the body remembers what families choose to forget
- Breaking the chains: interrupting inherited patterns

Table of Contents continued.

Part Two: The Body Keeps Score

How trauma manifests physically and shapes our relationships

Chapter 5: The Body's Ledger

- The nervous system's perfect memory
- Physical symptoms nobody connects to trauma
- The amygdala: your inner drama queen
- The vagus nerve: your body's information highway
- Hypervigilance: the exhausting superpower
- The immune system, gut, and the body's timeline

Chapter 6: Relationships as Mirrors

- How do we recreate childhood dynamics in adult relationships
- Attachment styles: secure, anxious, avoidant, and disorganised
- Trauma bonding and the addiction to chaos
- The body's wisdom in relationship choices
- Breaking patterns without breaking yourself

Chapter 7: The Masks We Wear

- Using humour and performance as survival strategies
- The physical toll of emotional masking
- The compassionate person in a desensitised world

Zelda Marsh

- Authenticity as a path to healing
- When the body says "enough" to pretending

Chapter 8: The Nervous System's Language

- The four F's of trauma response: Fight, Flight, Freeze, and Fawn
- Polyvagal Theory in everyday Northern English
- Triggers: when the past invades the present
- Dissociation: the ultimate escape hatch
- Somatic symptoms are the body's distress signals
- Co-regulation and healing in connection

PART THREE: RECLAMATION & HEALING

Finding freedom without forgiveness

Chapter 9: The Breaking Point

- The kitchen floor epiphany
- The body's ultimatum after years of ignored signals
- False starts in the healing journey
- Processing grief and rage
- The identity crisis that comes with healing
- Transforming your relationship with your body

Chapter 10: The Science of Healing

- Neuroplasticity (or "why I'm not still hiding in my bedroom")
- The Window of Tolerance (or "why I sometimes act like a complete Nutter")

- The Polyvagal Theory (or "why I'm not just being a drama queen")
- The Triune Brain (or "why my rational mind and emotional mind don't talk")
- The Science of Self-Compassion (or "why being kind to myself isn't just New Age bollocks")

Chapter 11: Forgiveness vs. Freedom

- The "forgiveness industrial complex" and how it traumatises survivors
- The toxic forgiveness trap
- Boundaries are more healing than forced forgiveness
- Self-forgiveness as distinct from forgiving others
- Acceptance as an alternative to forgiveness
- Finding freedom beyond the forgiveness narrative

Chapter 12: The Ongoing Journey

- The Myth of "Getting Over It" (Or Why Healing Isn't a Bloody Finish Line)
- The "Good Enough" Healing (Or Why Perfectionism Can Sod Right Off)
- Boundaries Without Forgiveness (Or, How to Tell People to Sod Off Without Feeling Guilty)
- The Healing Toolkit (Or, What to Do When You're Having a Shit Day)
- Finding Meaning Beyond Trauma (Without Spiritual Bypassing)

Conclusion: The Light Gets In

Zelda Marsh

- The myth of "completely healed"
- The body: from enemy to ally
- Boundaries: the unsung heroes of healing
- The freedom beyond forgiveness
- Finding light through the cracks

Epilogue: Where I Am Now
- The daily practice of being human
- The ripple effect of personal healing
- The journey of writing this book
- What comes next in the healing journey
- A final thank you

References
- Academic sources
- Additional resources
- Books for further reading
- Online resources and communities
- Somatic practices and movement therapies

PART ONE: THE WOUNDS
WHERE THE TRAUMA BEGINS.

Zelda Marsh

Chapter 1: Born Into Brokenness

The Science Behind Early Imprinting

Let me take you on a little journey. Buckle the eff up—this one's bumpy, grim, funny in the worst ways, and sacred in ways I didn't even realise I was living through at the time.

I came into this world already labelled. I was born with twisted legs and a medical chart thicker than most kids' bedtime stories. I couldn't walk until I was five. Until then, I had braces, boots, strange contraptions, and people in white coats talking like I wasn't there. NHS specials strapped me in like a malfunctioning baby robot. My earliest memories aren't cuddles; they're corridors, cold hands, and clinical words I didn't understand.

I don't remember being told I was broken. But I felt it. In every sideways glance. In the sighs of overworked doctors. In the way my mum's mouth tightened when she looked at me sometimes.

Before I had words, I had sensation. My body knew it was different before I did. I flinched before I understood fear. My nervous system was being trained for war while I was still in nappies.

The fancy researchers like Dr. Bruce Perry would tell you that when a baby experiences stress, even the kind that comes from medical procedures or feeling "different," their developing brain gets flooded with stress hormones. The amygdala, that little almond-shaped drama queen in your brain, gets hyperactive, while the prefrontal cortex, the rational bit supposed to say, "Chill out, we're safe," doesn't develop properly.

My brain was wired for danger before I could say "danger." My body was keeping score from day one.

And then came school. That's when I learned what others saw when they looked at me. Charlie Chaplin. Penguin. Spaz. Cruel names served up on playground tarmac with a side of fake kindness.

I laughed. Always laughed. Got in on the joke first. Because if I was laughing, they weren't tearing me apart. Not properly. Humour became my shield. Sarcasm was my armour. Performance? Survival.

Family Foundations: Shaky Ground

My parents? They were kids themselves, emotionally stunted and unhealed. They loved me, I think, in their way. But it was jagged, clumsy, and reactive. They passed me to my grandparents more times than I could count, like a hot potato wrapped in expectations and regret.

My grandparents weren't cruel; they were survivors. They did what survivors do: put the kettle on, carry on, don't ask, don't tell. We didn't talk about emotions. We made pies and cleaned things.

The Violation That Changed Everything

There's one memory that's stuck like Velcro on my soul. I was around six. A twelve-year-old boy anally raped me. It wasn't violent in the way people think of violence—there was no shouting, no dramatic struggle. But it was wrong—a boundary obliterated. A sacred part of me was violated in ways my young mind couldn't process, but my body would never forget.

I knew something terrible had happened. My body knew before my mind could form the words. I went to my mother instinctively, seeking safety and care. I remember her face changing as she realised something was wrong. But what came next wasn't protection. It wasn't justice. It wasn't even an acknowledgement.

Instead, I was passed around her friends like a parcel at a party game. Each one taking a look at "my bits," examining me with clinical curiosity while I stood there, humiliated, confused, exposed all over again. Their faces, their whispers, their looks of pity or disgust, I remember it all.

Zelda Marsh

And then? Nothing. Absolute bloody nothing. No police. No counselling. No conversations. No checking if I was okay. Just silence. As if it never happened. As if my body hadn't been turned into a crime scene. As if the pain I felt, physical and soul-deep, was just something to be tidied away like spilt tea.

My hips clenched, my shoulders froze, and I forgot how to exhale. My body knew what my mind couldn't yet comprehend: Something fundamental had been broken, and no one was going to help me fix it.

That's what people don't realise about trauma. It doesn't always come in screaming. Sometimes it whispers. It hides in politeness, in silence, in family rooms. And it stays in your body like an unpaid bill.

The Invisible Child Syndrome

I became the invisible child, not literally, though sometimes I wished for that superpower, but emotionally invisible. I was the good one, the responsible one, the one who never caused trouble.

According to Dr. Jonice Webb, who wrote about "Childhood Emotional Neglect," kids like me develop a particular kind of invisibility. We learn to take up less space, need less, want less, and feel less. We become emotional chameleons, blending into whatever environment we're in because standing out feels dangerous.

I was praised for being "so mature," "so helpful," "so put together." But inside, I was empty. My inner child was starving for softness, for someone to notice the weight I was carrying without ever asking for help.

School became my escape, sanctuary, and one place of safety and certainty. I wasn't the class clown; I was the prefect. The model student. The one who soaked up every bit of learning like it was air. I craved the stability, the routine, the sense of purpose. School was the only place I could fully focus on something other than survival. It was the sacred space where, for a few hours each day, I didn't have to live the chaos; I could just be.

The Body's Early Warning System

Looking back, it's obvious I was a walking trauma chart. Sexual abuse trauma? My body responded with chronic urinary tract infections, with unexplained stomach pains, with a disconnection from my physical self that would take decades to heal. Neglect trauma? I had low self-esteem before I even knew what self meant. I was the invisible kid, responsible, polite, never a problem, so I got ignored. Confidence trauma? I flinched at praise and expected rejection. I wore self-doubt like it was stitched into my skin. Guilt trauma? I'd apologise just for taking up space. I didn't ask for anything ever. It felt like asking meant someone might leave. And inner child trauma in general? I lived in fear. I hated being alone, but didn't know how to trust a connection either.

It was all unspoken, but it ran the show. I was emotionally starving, but I acted like I was fine. I couldn't set boundaries because I thought I had to earn love by not needing anything. I attracted emotionally unavailable people over and over again because that was the blueprint.

And none of this was "just in my head." This lived in my nervous system, in my digestion, in my posture, in my breath.

It was somatic trauma programming, and I'd been carrying it since I could barely walk. What no one told me back then, but my body knew the whole damn time was that trauma doesn't just live in memory. It lives in flesh.

All those years of flinching, freezing, and fawning? They rewired my brain, shrinking parts and supercharging others. My amygdala, that overworked little almond-shaped drama queen in my brain, was always screaming, "Danger!" while my prefrontal cortex sat in the corner, saying, "I'd like to think clearly, but we're under attack, babes."

It made me:

- Hyper-aware but exhausted

- Smart but scattered
- Funny but numb
- Energetic but constantly ready to shut down.

I didn't just have "moods"—I had chemical warfare in my system. My gut? A disaster. My immune system? Shot. Sleep? Forget it.

And that's what pisses me off—how we frame trauma like it's "all in your head." No. It's in your cells. It's in your vagus nerve. It's in your hormones, your cortisol spikes, your gut bacteria, your effing breath.

I wasn't lazy. I wasn't just being dramatic—though I might've been loud, fast, and a little theatrical at times, sure. But that was all wrapped up in a carefully curated mask. I was in survival mode for a decade straight, and no one noticed.

That's the impact of childhood trauma. Not just the pain of what happened. But the shame of carrying it alone and not even knowing why your body feels broken.

The Science of Childhood Sexual Trauma

Let's talk about what happens in a child's brain and body during sexual abuse, because understanding this helped me finally make sense of my own reactions.

Dr. Bessel van der Kolk explains that childhood sexual trauma creates what he calls "developmental trauma disorder." When a child is sexually abused, especially by someone older, and then has that trauma dismissed or ignored by caregivers, it creates a perfect storm of betrayal that affects every system in the body.

Zelda Marsh

The brain's threat-detection system goes into permanent overdrive. The body's stress response gets stuck in the "on" position. The child learns that their body isn't safe, that adults can't be trusted, and that their pain doesn't matter.

This explains why I developed chronic physical symptoms at such a young age. Why I dissociated from my body—floating above myself as if I weren't really there. We struggled with boundaries, trust, and intimacy, and I felt dirty, damaged, and different.

It wasn't just psychological—it was neurobiological. My entire nervous system was reorganised around this unprocessed trauma.

And the silence that followed? That "never speak of it again" approach? That compounded the damage. Now, I wasn't just carrying the trauma of what happened; I was carrying the message that it wasn't important enough to address, that my pain wasn't worth acknowledging, that the violation of my body was something to be hidden, not healed.

This is what researchers call "betrayal trauma"—when the people who should protect you either cause harm or fail to respond to damage caused by others. It's a double wound. And it changes not just how you see the world, but how your body operates within it.

But here's the twist—this wasn't just my trauma. It was ancestral.

I didn't grow up in a vacuum. I grew up in the aftermath of generations who were told to hush, to suffer quietly, to stay married, to drink the pain away, never to rock the boat.

My grandma never spoke about feelings. She baked them into pies, carried them in her back, and tucked them into silence. I only recently found out she'd lost her first husband in the war, missing in action, they said. Then, left with nine children and no support, she had to put them into care because she couldn't cope. Her mother, a Welsh herbalist, had moved her to England as a child. That grief, that resilience, that history? It lived in her bones. And she passed it down, quiet as breath.

And my dad? It turns out he'd been pulled from pillar to post between my nana, her husband, and her ex-husband. The man he thought was his dad, Walter, a big bloke with a limp from polio who'd been found in a basket on a doorstep as a baby, wasn't actually his biological father. His real dad was my nana's first husband, who was deaf like she was. And if that wasn't enough chaos, my dad also spent time in care homes himself. His personal claim to fame? Apparently, he once shared a room in a nun-run care home with none other than John Lennon. Trauma and rock 'n' roll run deep in the bloodline.

My dad never healed his pain; he passed it down like a cursed heirloom. And me? I inherited it all. The grief, the fear, the rage that didn't belong to me, but clung like skin.

I didn't have the language back then. But my body knew.

The First Whispers of Something More

I didn't realise it then, but humour was my first spiritual tool. It protected me, transmuted pain, and kept me human when I felt like a ghost.

Zelda Marsh

But god, the cost of being "the strong one." No one checks on the strong one. No one hugs the strong one. The strong one never gets a day off.

The truth is: being strong is effing exhausting.

I was clairsentient before I knew the word. I used to have dreams that felt more real than waking life. Sometimes, it was people I didn't recognise but felt like I knew. Sometimes, it was messages I didn't understand until years later. And sometimes, it was just a feeling—like someone was watching, but not in a creepy way—more like, "We've got you."

I'd see animals that weren't supposed to be there. Blackbirds on the windowsill, staring like they had something to say. A fox that sat still and watched me cry once when I ran out into the garden. Butterflies showing up in winter. And the etchings on the glass created through the frosting of ice? Now those were magical—like sacred messages from the universe carved in crystal code, just for me.

Coincidence? Maybe. But deep down, I knew—I wasn't alone.

Back then, I didn't know the word "Spirit," what "clairsentient" meant, or what guides, energy, or ancestral presence meant.

But I felt them. Every tingle. Every intuitive "nope." Every goosebump that said pay attention. And sometimes—sometimes it was that piercing, high-pitched tone in my ear, like the kind that could shatter glass. A frequency so sharp and sudden it felt like a cosmic dog whistle, reminding me I wasn't alone.

I Don't Need Your Forgiveness To Heal

It was like my soul had been handed a satnav, but no one gave me the map. And still, I trusted it, even when I thought I was making it up, even when the world told me it was nonsense. I followed the breadcrumbs. I listened anyway.

I felt it all before it ever landed. I walked into rooms and knew when something was off. I woke up from dreams that weren't mine. I got sick when others were angry. I thought I was just "too sensitive." Turns out, I was tuned in.

Spirit was whispering to me before I even knew how to listen. I used to see shadows move when no one was there. I'd get sudden chills and know someone was watching, but not in a scary way. In a familiar way. Like they were there to guide me, not haunt me.

I didn't have sage, rituals, or language for any of it. But I had instinct. I had goosebumps, gut feelings, and dreams I couldn't explain.

I remember once sitting at the top of the stairs, crying quietly. I was probably seven. No one knew. No one saw. But I swear to you, I felt someone put their hand on my back. Gentle. Warm. Real. And then I stood up and carried on. Because that's what I always did, and it still happens to this day. That presence, whatever or whoever it is, has never left. It offers me more protection, trust, and support than any human ever has. A quiet, sacred force that reminds me I'm never truly alone.

But now I know I wasn't just surviving. I was being guided.

Zelda Marsh

Reflection: The Seeds of Strength

Looking back at that little girl with the twisted legs, the violated body, and the too-big heart, I don't feel pity. I feel awe. Because despite it all, despite the medical trauma, the sexual abuse, the betrayal by those who should have protected me, the emotional neglect, the playground cruelty, she kept going. She found ways to matter. She created value where she could. She learned to read rooms before she could read books. She developed empathy as a survival skill.

She wasn't broken. She was becoming.

And that's the thing about early wounds, they don't just leave scars. They leave superpowers. Hypervigilance? That's also intuition. People-pleasing? That's also empathy. Dissociation? That's also imagination.

The very things that hurt us can become our greatest strengths—if we learn how to transmute them.

But first, we have to acknowledge them. Feel them. Name them. Own them.

And that's what this chapter is about, not wallowing in the past and not playing victim. But it recognises that we must know what we're healing from before we can truly heal.

So here I am, acknowledging it all. The twisted legs. The cold corridors. The sexual violation. The betrayal of silence. The whispered cruelties. The invisible child syndrome. The body that knew before the mind could comprehend.

This is where it started. This is the foundation, shaky as it was, on which everything else was built.

But this isn't where it ends. Not by a long shot.

Because that little girl with the NHS boots and the too-wise eyes? She grew up to be me. And I'm still here. Still standing. Still laughing, but now, it's not just to survive. It's because I've earned every effing chuckle.

And that's a story worth telling.

Reflection Prompt: What early experiences shaped your body's response to the world? Can you feel where your first wounds still live in your physical form? What would it be like to acknowledge them without judgment?

Zelda Marsh

Chapter 2: Abandonment & Its Aftermath

The Invisible Wound That Shapes Everything

When I was around eight, my mum left. She packed up her life and didn't include me in it. She went off with a new bloke, one who already had two kids. I was left behind like spare luggage, something she couldn't take with her because it didn't fit the new décor.

That kind of abandonment doesn't just break your heart, it rewires your effing nervous system.

Talk about what maternal abandonment actually does to a child's developing brain, shall we? Because it's not just about feeling sad or missing your mum's cooking.

According to attachment theory (cheers, John Bowlby), when a primary caregiver, especially a mother, leaves, it creates what therapists call "primal abandonment trauma." It's not just emotional; it's physiological. Your brain literally develops differently. Your stress response system goes into overdrive. Your ability to trust gets fundamentally altered.

Dr. Gabor Maté explains it like this: when a child is abandoned, their brain interprets it as a survival threat. Not just "Mum's gone," but "I might die." Evolutionarily speaking, without a caregiver, a child wouldn't survive. So, my little eight-year-old brain wasn't being dramatic; it was responding exactly as it was designed to.

And here's the kicker: This response doesn't just go away when you grow up. It becomes the foundation for how you approach every relationship, every challenge, and every bloody Tuesday for the rest of your life.

Zelda Marsh

Becoming the Mum at Eight

At eight, I became the mum, not just to myself but to my siblings. I cooked pasta, wiped noses, folded socks, and listened for fights while pretending I didn't need anyone. I played caregiver, comedian, and keeper of calm.

Dad was a ghost with fists. Sometimes funny. Sometimes frightening. You never knew which version you'd get, or what would set him off. He didn't speak in feelings but in door slams and silence. Booze was his love language. Rage was his lullaby.

I became an expert in emotional weather. I could read a room like radar. I could tell by the way he dropped his keys if it was going to be a stormy night. Hypervigilance? That's the technical term. I just called it living.

Every night, I'd go to bed in a ball. Muscles locked. Jaw clenched. Listening and always listening. Would there be shouting? Would something break? Would someone leave again?

That's what trauma does. It teaches your body to anticipate danger. To scan the horizon constantly. It turns your ribcage into a cage. Your stomach becomes a war drum.

The Physical Toll of Emotional Absence

Trauma expert Bessel van der Kolk says the body keeps the score. Mine was keeping a detailed, bloody ledger.

My shoulders? Permanently hunched, braced for impact. My digestion? A disaster zone, irritable bowel syndrome by age ten, though no one called it that then. My sleep? Fractured, light, always ready to jump up if needed. My immune system? Constantly compromised colds, infections, and mysterious rashes that doctors dismissed as "stress-related."

Because here's what happens when you're in a constant state of fight-or-flight: your body diverts resources away from "non-essential" functions like digestion, immune response, and growth. It's all hands-on deck for survival, love.

I developed migraines at nine. Insomnia at ten. Chronic stomach pain that no one could explain. My body was screaming what my mouth couldn't say: "I'm not okay. I'm carrying too much. Someone, please notice."

But no one did. Or if they did, they didn't know what to do with it. So, I kept going, kept smiling, and kept pretending that being "mature for my age" was a compliment rather than a symptom.

Brother Lost, Guilt Found

And let's not forget—right around this time, while my new baby brother was being doted on, my **real** brother, the one who survived all the chaos with me, was ripped from our world and dumped into care and branded as too much. Too feral. Too angry. But what did they expect?

He was hurting. He didn't know how to process the mess of emotions inside him, let alone express them. No one taught him how. No one stopped long enough to say, "Hey, are you alright?"

He was a boy carrying bombs inside his chest, and still, he was just a child. A child who needed holding, not fixing. A child who needed gentleness, not judgement. A child who needed someone to sit in the pain with him, not send him away.

While I watched a new life get celebrated, I silently grieved the boy I grew up with being erased from the narrative. And me? I wasn't sure where I fit anymore.

And part of me never forgave myself for surviving when he didn't get the chance to.

The guilt of being the one who stayed, the one who adapted, the one who wasn't "too much" lived in my chest like a stone. I carried it everywhere. Still do, if I'm honest.

The Science of Generational Trauma

This isn't just family drama, it's epigenetics. Research shows that trauma can actually alter gene expression, passing down not just behaviours but biological responses to stress. Dr. Rachel Yehuda's research on Holocaust survivors and their descendants found that children of traumatised parents had different cortisol levels and stress responses than children whose parents hadn't experienced severe trauma.

In plain English? The way my body responds to stress, the racing heart, the knotted stomach, the constant vigilance, isn't just because of what happened to me. It's also because of what happened to my dad, my grandma, and generations before them.

Their unprocessed pain became my biological inheritance. Their silence became my screaming nervous system.

Early Spiritual Connections: The Unseen Support

I was clairsentient before I knew the word. I used to have dreams that felt more real than waking life. Sometimes, it was people I didn't recognise but felt like I knew. Sometimes, it was messages I didn't understand until years later. And sometimes, it was just a feeling like someone was watching, but not in a creepy way, more like, "We've got you."

I'd see animals that weren't supposed to be there. Blackbirds on the windowsill, staring like they had something to say. A fox that sat still and watched me cry once when I ran out into the garden. Butterflies showing up in winter. And the etchings on the glass created through the frosting of ice? Now those were magical—like sacred messages from the universe carved in crystal code, just for me.

Coincidence? Maybe. But deep down, I knew I wasn't alone.

Back then, I didn't know the word "Spirit," what "clairsentient" meant, or what guides, energy, or ancestral presence meant.

But I felt them. Every tingle. Every intuitive "nope." Every goosebump that said pay attention. And sometimes, it was that piercing, high-pitched tone in my ear, like the kind that could shatter glass. A frequency so sharp and sudden it felt like a cosmic dog whistle, reminding me I wasn't alone.

It was like my soul had been handed a satnav, but no one gave me the map. And still, I trusted it even when I thought I was making it up, even when the world told me it was nonsense. I followed the breadcrumbs. I listened anyway.

I felt it all before it ever landed. I walked into rooms and knew when something was off. I woke up from dreams that weren't mine. I got sick when others were angry. I thought I was just "too sensitive." Turns out, I was tuned in.

Spirit was whispering to me before I even knew how to listen. I used to see shadows move when no one was there. I'd get sudden chills and know someone was watching, but not in a scary way. In a familiar way. Like they were there to guide me, not haunt me.

I Don't Need Your Forgiveness To Heal

I didn't have sage, rituals, or language for any of it. But I had instinct. I had goosebumps, gut feelings, and dreams I couldn't explain.

I remember once sitting at the top of the stairs, crying quietly. I was probably seven. No one knew. No one saw. But I swear to you, I felt someone put their hand on my back. Gentle. Warm. Real. And then I stood up and carried on. Because that's what I always did, and it still happens to this day. That presence, whatever or whoever it is, has never left. It offers me more protection, trust, and support than any human ever has. A quiet, sacred force that reminds me I'm never truly alone.

But now I know I wasn't just surviving, I was being guided, I wasn't just making it up as I went along; I

And then came the day. The moment. Not a breakdown. Not a scream. Not a lightning strike. Just a quiet, sacred vow from somewhere deep in my chest that said: "This ends with me."

I knew then, without a doubt, that I wasn't meant to carry this pain forward. I was meant to break it apart. Burn it. Bury it. Transmute it.

So, my children would never have to carry what I did. Their children would know love without fear, and my bloodline could breathe again.

I remember the exact moment I knew I wasn't going to pass this pain on. I was standing in the kitchen. My youngest was crying. I was triggered, shaking, holding back the urge to scream, but I didn't. Instead, I dropped to the floor. Literally, I sat, cross-legged, right there on the cold tiles, holding myself like I wish someone had held me.

Zelda Marsh

And I said out loud, my voice shaking, my eyes stinging, "**It ends with me**. I'm not doing this to them."

I'd never said it before. But I knew it wasn't just a promise. It was a spell. An invocation. A contract sealed in sweat, tears, and maternal fury.

That moment? That's when I realised: I wasn't weak. I wasn't broken. I was the first one in the bloodline brave enough to feel it all.

The Body's Wisdom in Abandonment

What's fascinating about abandonment trauma is how the body responds to it differently than other types of trauma. With physical trauma, the body often freezes or dissociates. But with abandonment? The body goes into a complex dance of hypervigilance and collapse.

Dr. Peter Levine, who developed Somatic Experiencing therapy, explains that abandonment creates a unique trauma response: the body simultaneously prepares to fight for connection and surrenders to the impossibility of getting it. It's like pressing the accelerator and the brake at the same time.

This explains why, as a child, I was both fiercely independent ("I don't need anyone") and desperately clingy (terrified when people I loved were out of sight). My nervous system was caught in a terrible contradiction, reaching out and pulling back, seeking connection and expecting rejection all at once.

It's why I developed what therapists call an "anxious-avoidant attachment style", wanting closeness but fearing it, needing connection but running from it, loving deeply but always with one foot out the door.

My body was trying to protect me from the pain of being left again, but doing so created patterns that made a genuine connection nearly impossible.

Reflection: The Strength in Acknowledging Abandonment

The thing about abandonment is that we're taught to minimise it. "Lots of kids have divorced parents." "At least you weren't abused." "Your mum had her own issues to deal with."

But abandonment is a profound wound. It shapes your sense of self, your belief in your worthiness, and your capacity for trust. It's not something to brush off or power through.

Acknowledging the depth of this wound isn't wallowing in it; it's wisdom. It's saying, "This happened, and it mattered, and it changed me." It's the first step toward healing.

Because here's what I know now that I didn't know then: the abandoned child doesn't have to become the abandoned adult. The patterns can be broken. The wounds can be tended. The body can learn new responses.

But first, we have to name it. Feel it. Honour it.

So, I'm naming it now. I was abandoned. And it hurt. And it changed me. And it's okay to say that.

It's also okay to say that I survived it, that I found strength in it, and that I developed resilience, intuition, and empathy because of it.

Abandonment didn't define me, but it did shape me. And recognising that shape is the first step toward reshaping it into something of my own choosing.

Reflection Prompt: Where do you feel the echo of abandonment or rejection in your body? What physical sensations arise when you think about times you were left behind or pushed away? Can you sit with those sensations with compassion rather than judgment?

I Don't Need Your Forgiveness To Heal

Chapter 3: Teenage Turmoil

Zelda Marsh

Running Away at Fourteen

Ahh, the teenage years. That was the golden era of awkward haircuts, bad decisions, and enough emotional chaos to rival a soap opera marathon.

Spoiler alert: mine wasn't exactly a dream sequence.

I ran away from my dad's house at 14, not out of rebellion, but because I felt like I'd been quietly voted off the family island. He'd had a significant health scare, and my stepmum (only five years older than me, by the way) suddenly became the full-time Carer, nurse, new mum, and emotional gatekeeper. She'd just had a baby, my new little brother, and the dynamic shifted overnight. It should've been a time of joy, right? But for me, it came with the hollow ache of loss.

Gone were the cuddles, the inside jokes, the feeling of being anyone's priority.

At first, I tried to adjust. I tiptoed, helped out, and played along. I even gently asked how he was coping. I wasn't confrontational, I was compassionate. I asked if he needed anything, if he was okay, and if there was anything I could do. But my care was invisible, irrelevant.

She would glance past me, sigh at my presence. I felt like a piece of furniture no one wanted to sit on anymore. The atmosphere grew cold, clipped, and sharp with unspoken rules I didn't know I was breaking. My dad was fragile. She was in charge. And I was... inconvenient.

She didn't know how to play 'stepmum,' and to be honest, she didn't seem interested in trying. I became the misplaced jigsaw piece no one knew where to put—awkward, ghost-like, and expected to disappear quietly.

And then one day, after yet another tense silence and side-eye over breakfast, I snapped. Not loudly. Not dramatically. Quietly. Silently. Internally. I decided I couldn't stay another day in a house where I was seen but not felt, where I was tolerated but not loved.

So off I popped, after sneaking out of school and hiding in a small town all day, a little teenage fugitive, absolutely bursting with fear and a full bladder. I wet myself on the bus ride to my mum's—I was that scared. Scared of being caught. Afraid of doing something "wrong." Fearful of upsetting my dad. But mostly, I was scared of what the hell I was walking into.

Zelda Marsh

The Trauma of Displacement

What I didn't understand then, but research makes clear now, is that this kind of displacement creates what psychologists call "developmental trauma." It's not just about losing your home; it's about losing your place in the world, your sense of belonging, your fundamental security.

Dr. Bruce Perry, a leading researcher in childhood trauma, explains that adolescence is already a time of massive brain reorganisation. The teenage brain prunes connections, builds new ones, and essentially remodels itself for adulthood. When trauma hits during this critical period, it doesn't just create emotional distress; it literally shapes how the brain develops.

My teenage brain was trying to figure out identity, sexuality, future plans, all the usual adolescent stuff, while simultaneously processing rejection, displacement, and the shattering of family bonds. No bloody wonder I was a mess.

And the physical symptoms? Classic trauma response. The fear was so intense that I lost control of my bladder. That's the autonomic nervous system in overdrive—fight, flight, or freeze taken to its extreme. My body was literally saying, "This is too much. I can't hold it together anymore."

From Frying Pan to Fire

And let me tell you, walking into that house wasn't exactly a warm hug from the Universe. Within days, I'd been upgraded from "daughter" to live-in help. Nanny, housemaid, general dogsbody. All for free. Cheers, Mum.

Oh, and she'd shackled up with a new fella with two kids of his own, charming. Nothing says welcome back like watching your mother play happy families with someone else's children while you're busy being her emotional and let's be genuine, physical punching bag.

Yeah, that happened. That house was where I first learned that shame, guilt and unresolved mother wounds can show up in fists. She was dealing with her mess, I get it now, but at the time, I caught it: the guilt, the blame, the violence. I still flinch at the memory of having my head cracked against that bloody artexed wall (you remember the ones plastered with extra lumps for decorative torture). Neck pain? Yeah. I've still got that lousy son of a biatch living with me.

But I kept going. Because what else do you do when your nervous system's wired for survival?

The Pregnancy That Wasn't Mine to Carry Alone

And then him. He came. Older. Smooth-talking. He was a taxi driver, I know, babe, at seventeen, I knew how to pull 'em, and he appeared at the right moment. I was seventeen, moving out of my grandma's and into my flat. It was a fresh start, a new chapter. But I didn't know that it also made me the perfect candidate. I was a bit lost, a bit lonely, just looking for something that felt like love.

By the time I was pregnant, I wasn't even living at my mum's anymore; she'd kicked me out at sixteen. Threw hot black coffee at me, burned my pale blue outfit, and watched me run down the alley with more than just stained clothes. I carried that moment with me, all the way into a toxic relationship and a bed that never felt like mine.

The night I lost my virginity wasn't a rite of passage. It was a ritual of resignation. I bathed for what felt like hours, scrubbing, crying, and trying to wash off the wrongness. But it clung to me. Lived in me.

Then came him, the taxi driver. He was older, charming, and smiling like salvation. He helped me move into my first flat, flirted while lifting boxes, and made me feel like maybe I was wanted, not just tolerated.

I didn't see the warning signs until I was already too deep. Too flattered. Too flung wide open.

And when the warts showed up? I felt filthier than I've ever felt in my life. Burned off in secret and treated alone. I couldn't even look the nurse in the eye. I told them I was in a committed relationship, as if that would justify the shame. As if that would make me clean again.

Then I found out I was pregnant. And for a brief, breathless second, I thought I could handle it. That may be the moment I turned it all around.

I Don't Need Your Forgiveness To Heal

Until she opened her mouth. My mother. With her ever-sharp sixth sense and no filter, she just looked at me and said:

"You're pregnant, aren't you?"

I didn't even get to say yes. Because before I could blink, she told him. She told him I was pregnant. My choice. My body. My moment. And she took it and handed it off like gossip in an effing pub.

He showed up that night with the words that would live in my gut forever:

"So.. what are you going to do about it?"

I remember sitting across from him as he laid it out like some polite suggestion: how "living with his sister" made it impossible, how we were "too young," and how the timing was just... bad.

But the worst part? It wasn't just that he wanted me to get rid of the pregnancy. It was the way he said it. Like I'd spilt milk. Like it was an inconvenience. Like, I was the problem.

And I was so numb, so worn down by trying to make sense of other people's choices, I let his words sink in like gospel. I didn't fight. I folded.

He said he'd pay, he'd go with me, we'd start again, and he said all the right things—until he didn't show up again.

The procedure took place on April 9th, 1985. I remember the date because it felt like time had stopped.

Zelda Marsh

I remember lying on that table, tears sliding silently into my ears, whispering, "No... no, I've changed my mind..." but no one listened, stopped, or heard me.

And so, I did what I always did: shut down and survived it.

I walked out of that clinic hollow, not because of the decision, but because it was never entirely mine.

And when I needed support the most? My mother, who had betrayed my confidence, turned around and disowned me for going through with it.

The woman who told the secret was now shaming me for what it cost.

And still I survived. My body kept going. My heart kept beating. My story kept moving forward. But part of me froze that day. Part of me stayed on that table, waiting for someone to say, "You're allowed to grieve finally."

That part? I write for her now. Because no girl should have to carry silence where her rage belongs, no woman should feel filthy for someone else's lies.

And I'll be damned if I let that story die with shame still clinging to it.

That version of me, the one who walked out of that clinic and kept going? She was never weak. She was surviving the only way she knew how.

The Body's Response to Reproductive Trauma

What happened to me wasn't just emotionally devastating—it was physically traumatic in ways I'm only now beginning to understand.

Dr. Judith Herman, a pioneer in trauma research, identifies what she calls "complex trauma", the kind that happens when you experience multiple violations of autonomy, especially at the hands of people who should protect you. My mother's betrayal of confidence, the boyfriend's abandonment, and the medical procedure where my "no" was ignored created a perfect storm of complex trauma.

And my body responded accordingly. After the procedure, I developed chronic pelvic pain that no doctor could explain. My periods became erratic, painful, and debilitating. I had recurring infections, as if my body was trying to fight off an invasion that had already happened.

But the most profound physical response was dissociation, that floating feeling, like I wasn't really in my body anymore, like I was watching myself from somewhere else. Researchers now understand this as a protective mechanism. When the body experiences something too overwhelming, it creates distance. It's saying, "This is too much to process right now. We'll step away and come back when it's safer."

Except I didn't come back. Not fully. Not for years. I stayed slightly removed from my physical self, present but not present, here but not here. It was safer that way.

The body remembers what the mind tries to forget. And mine remembered everything.

Zelda Marsh

Your Body Never Forgets, And Mine Was Screaming

Let's get one thing straight, love your body is not just some meat suit you're dragging around. She's a whole effing library of everything you've ever been through. Every time someone hurt you, ignored you, or made you shrink? Yeah, she logged it.

For years, I thought I was just "sensitive." I couldn't handle a raised voice, got jumpy when someone slammed a door and had a stomach that tied itself in knots over nothing.

Except it wasn't nothing.

It was everything.

It turns out that your nervous system can't tell the difference between your dad shouting in 1995 and your boss sending a blunt email in 2023. It just goes: *Danger!*

And boom, your heart's racing, you've lost your appetite, and you're crying in the toilet like you've just been dumped. Again.

That's what Dr. Gabor Maté calls "trauma imprinting." It's your past stuck on repeat in your body.

And here's where Bessel van der Kolk comes in again: The Body Keeps Score! That title hit me like a slap. It's not just a book; it's a bloody diagnosis.

It's why your back seizes up before family Christmas. It's also why your shoulders feel like concrete every Monday.

And why does your gut act like it's running from a sabre-toothed tiger when you're just standing in Tesco?

It's not your fault, love. It's your body doing what it has to do to survive.

Trauma Bingo: How Many Boxes Did You Tick Before Breakfast?

Let's play a game. It's called: "Bloody Hell, No Wonder I'm Like This."

Also known as: The ACE Test (Adverse Childhood Experiences, for those new to this rollercoaster.)

This isn't about self-pity. This is context. Because when you grow up with chaos in your DNA, you start thinking the chaos is you.

Here's the official list—tick 'em off like trauma-based Top Trumps:

1. Emotional abuse
2. Physical abuse
3. Sexual abuse
4. Emotional neglect
5. Physical neglect
6. Parental separation or divorce
7. Domestic violence in the home
8. Substance abuse in the household
9. Mental illness in the household
10. A household member who was incarcerated

How many did you tick?

3? You're not alone.

5? Welcome to the club.

8+? Babe, you're an effing survivor wrapped in mascara and nervous system scars.

And here's the kicker: The higher your ACE score, the higher your risk of pretty much everything from anxiety to autoimmune issues to addiction and beyond.

But here's what they don't always say clearly: *You are not broken.*

Your body is reacting exactly how it's supposed to in a world that didn't know how to hold you.

You weren't born "difficult." You were just trained to survive the battlefield you were born into.

And now? Now you're not surviving. You're rewriting the effing map.

The Teenage Brain on Trauma

There's something fierce about trauma during the teenage years. Neuroscience tells us that the adolescent brain is going through a massive renovation project—pruning away unused connections, strengthening important ones, and essentially rewiring itself for adulthood.

When trauma hits during this critical period, it's like having a fire during a home renovation. The damage isn't just to what's already built—it's to the blueprint itself.

Dr. Daniel Siegel, a clinical professor of psychiatry, explains that trauma during adolescence can actually change how the brain develops. The prefrontal cortex—

responsible for rational thinking, planning, and emotional regulation—is particularly vulnerable.

This explains why, as a teenager dealing with displacement, violence, and reproductive trauma, I developed such extreme coping mechanisms. My brain was literally being shaped by these experiences, creating neural pathways that said, "The world is dangerous. People will hurt you. Don't trust. Don't relax. Don't feel."

It wasn't weakness or character flaws. It was neurobiology. My teenage brain was doing exactly what it was designed to do: adapt to survive.

The problem is, those adaptations that helped me survive as a teenager became maladaptive as an adult. The hypervigilance that kept me safe from my mother's unpredictable rage made intimate relationships nearly impossible. The emotional shutdown that protected me during the abortion left me disconnected from my own feelings for decades.

Understanding this isn't about making excuses, it's about having compassion for that teenage girl who was doing her best with a brain still under construction.

Reflection: Honouring the Teenage Survivor

Looking back at my teenage self, I don't see a victim. I see a bloody warrior.

A girl who, despite everything, kept going. Who found ways to laugh. Who dreamed of something better? Who survived not just physical blows but the deeper wounds of betrayal, abandonment, and violation.

Zelda Marsh

She wasn't broken, she was adapting. She wasn't difficult; she was responding to a difficult world. She wasn't too much, she was exactly what she needed to be to survive.

And now, decades later, I can finally say what no one told her: "I see you. I honour you. Your pain matters. Your resilience matters. You did the best you could with what you had."

That teenage girl carried profound wounds that would shape her adult life. But she also carried seeds of strength that would eventually bloom into healing.

The journey from there to here wasn't linear, it wasn't pretty, and it wasn't the kind of transformation story that fits neatly into an Instagram caption.

It was messy. It was painful. It took decades. And it's still ongoing.

But that's the thing about healing: It doesn't erase the wounds. It transforms them, gives them meaning, and turns them from liabilities into assets.

That teenage girl who survived so much? She's still here. In my quick laugh when things get tense. In my ability to read a room in seconds. In my fierce protection of those I love. In my refusal to accept bullshit or play small.

She's not a part of me I need to overcome or silence. She's a part of me I need to honour and integrate.

Because without her, without her pain, resilience, and refusal to give up, I wouldn't be who I am today.

I Don't Need Your Forgiveness To Heal

And who I am today is someone who can finally tell her story without shame, feel her feelings without drowning in them, and look back with compassion instead of judgment.

That's not just healing. That's reclamation.

Reflection Prompt: Think about your teenage years. What physical sensations arise when you remember that time? Where in your body do you feel the echoes of those experiences?

Can you place a hand on that part of your body and acknowledge, "I see you. I feel you. You carried so much."

Chapter 4 Ancestral Patterns: The Inherited Trauma

The Ghosts We Carry

I used to think my issues were just my own—like I'd somehow managed to cock up my life all by myself. Brilliant achievement, that. Give yourself a pat on the back, love. But then I started noticing these eerie similarities between my reactions and my mum's. The way we both freeze when someone raises their voice. How we both apologise when someone bumps into us. The constant feeling we need to make ourselves smaller, less visible, less... well, just less.

It wasn't just a coincidence. It was like I'd inherited her trauma responses along with her dodgy knees and inability to wink without looking like I'm having some facial spasm.

Turns out, trauma doesn't just live in the person who experienced it. It's the unwanted family heirloom nobody asked for, but everyone got stuck with it anyway. Your gran insists "must stay in the family", like that hideous porcelain figurine, even though it gives everyone nightmares.

The science backs this up, by the way. I'm not just being dramatic (though I do excel at that too—another family trait, cheers Mum). Research into epigenetics shows that trauma can alter gene expression, which can be passed down to future generations. Dr. Rachel Yehuda's research with Holocaust survivors and their children found that both groups had similar abnormalities in their stress hormone levels, despite the children never experiencing the Holocaust themselves.

So when I jump at loud noises or feel sick when someone's angry, I'm not just reacting to my own experiences. I'm carrying the echo of my mother's trauma, my grandmother's trauma, and possibly generations before them. It's like having a chorus of anxious ancestors all screaming safety tips in your ear at once.

"Don't trust him!" "Keep your head down!" "Make yourself useful or they'll discard you!" "Never show weakness!"

Bloody exhausting, that lot.

The Family Tree of Dysfunction

My family tree isn't just a record of births, marriages, and deaths. It's a map of trauma patterns, repeating themselves with depressing regularity, like some toxic family tradition.

My grandmother was abandoned by her mother and raised by relatives who made it clear she was a burden. My mother was emotionally neglected by my grandmother, who didn't have the tools to parent effectively. And then there's me, with my mother, who did her absolute best but worked from a broken instruction manual.

It's like each generation handed down a slightly modified version of the same wound. "Here you go, love. I've put my own special twist on this trauma. Enjoy!"

The pattern is painfully obvious when you step back and look at it:

Generation 1: Abandonment

Generation 2: Emotional neglect

Generation 3: Anxious attachment (that's me, waving awkwardly)

Each generation tried to do better than the last, but without healing the original wounds, we just created variations on the same theme. It's like trying to build a house on a cracked foundation. You can make it look pretty on the outside, but the structure is still compromised.

Dr. Mark Wolynn, author of "It Didn't Start With You," explains that family trauma patterns often repeat until someone becomes conscious of them and does the work to break the cycle. He writes, "The past is never dead. It's not even past." (That was William Faulkner, but Wolynn quotes him, so I'm counting it.)

The women in my family have a particular talent for finding emotionally unavailable partners. It's like we have radar for people who will confirm our deepest fear: that we are, fundamentally, unlovable. My grandmother married a man who worked away for months at a time. My mother chose my father, who was physically present but emotionally AWOL. And me? Well, I've had a string of relationships with people who could give masterclasses in avoidance and ambivalence.

Coincidence? Not bloody likely.

Zelda Marsh

The Body Remembers What the Family Forgets

Here's the truly bizarre part: sometimes we're carrying trauma that nobody even talks about. The big family secrets, the "we don't discuss that" events, the shame that's so deep it doesn't even have words attached to it anymore.

My maternal grandmother never spoke about her childhood. It was off-limits, a conversational no-go zone. But her body told the story, and her words wouldn't. The way she flinched when someone moved too quickly. How she hoarded food even when the cupboards were full. The insomnia that plagued her until her death.

Her body remembered what her family had collectively agreed to forget.

And then there's me, with my inexplicable fear of confined spaces, despite having no memory of being trapped anywhere. The panic rises when someone stands behind me. The way my throat closes up when I try to ask for what I need.

Where did these reactions come from? Some might be from my own experiences, sure. But others feel older, like they belong to someone else. They feel inherited.

In his groundbreaking book "The Body Keeps the Score," Dr. Bessel van der Kolk explains that trauma is stored in somatic memory and expressed through the body. Even if we have no conscious recollection of the traumatic events—either because we've suppressed them or because they happened to our ancestors—our bodies still react.

It's like my body is fluent in a language my mind doesn't even speak.

I remember sitting in therapy, trying to explain this strange feeling that some of my fears weren't actually mine.

"I know this sounds mental," I said, "but sometimes I feel like I'm afraid of things that never happened to me."

My therapist didn't laugh or reach for the referral form to the psychiatric unit. Instead, she nodded and said, "That's actually quite common. We call it inherited trauma or intergenerational trauma."

Well, brilliant. Another thing to add to the family inheritance. Couldn't we have passed down something useful instead, like property or money? But no, we got trauma patterns. Thanks a bunch, ancestors.

The Northern English Art of Not Talking About It

Of course, being from Northern England added another delightful layer to this ancestral trauma cake. We don't just carry trauma; we carry it silently, with a stiff upper lip and a cup of tea.

"How are you?" "Fine." "How's your mental health after discovering generations of trauma patterns in your family?" "Yeah, not bad. Fancy a brew?"

We're experts at not talking about the very things we most need to discuss. It's our superpower, passed down alongside the trauma itself—a double whammy of dysfunction.

Zelda Marsh

My family could sit through an entire Sunday dinner with tension so thick you could cut it with a knife, and nobody would acknowledge it. We'd pass the Yorkshire puddings with tight smiles and talk about the weather while carefully avoiding any topic of actual significance.

This culture of silence is the perfect breeding ground for trauma to flourish across generations. If we don't talk about it, we can't heal it. And if we can't heal it, we pass it on.

Dr. Joy DeGruy coined the term "Post Traumatic Slave Syndrome" to describe how the trauma of slavery continues to affect African Americans today, generations later. While my family's trauma isn't comparable to the horrors of slavery, the mechanism of transmission is similar. Trauma that isn't processed doesn't just disappear; it goes underground and emerges in the next generation.

In my family, the unspoken rule was: "If you don't talk about it, it didn't happen." Except it did happen, and our bodies knew it, even if our words denied it.

I remember my mother's hands shaking when certain topics came up. I remember the sudden changes in the subject, the awkward silences, and the warning glances. As a child, I learned to navigate these invisible boundaries without ever being told they existed.

"Don't ask about Grandma's parents." "Don't mention Uncle David." "Never ask why Dad leaves the room when war films come on."

These unspoken rules were as much a part of my inheritance as my eye colour or my inability to sing in tune.

Breaking the Bloody Cycle

So, there I was, carrying not just my own trauma but the unresolved trauma of generations before me. A walking archive of family wounds. What a delightful thought.

But here's the thing about recognising ancestral patterns: you can't unsee them once you see them. And once you can't unsee them, you have a choice to make. You can continue the pattern, or you can be the one who breaks the cycle.

I decided I didn't want to be another link in this chain of trauma. I didn't want to pass these patterns down to anyone else, whether that meant my own children or just the people who had the misfortune of getting close to me.

Breaking the cycle isn't easy, mind you. It's like trying to change the course of a river that's been flowing the same way for centuries. It requires constant awareness, consistent effort, and a willingness to feel incredibly uncomfortable as you forge a new path.

Dr. Gabor Maté, in his work on addiction and trauma, emphasises that healing requires us to face the very pain we've been running from. He writes, "The attempt to escape from pain is what creates more pain."

So instead of running from my ancestral patterns, I had to turn and face them. I had to look at the ways my grandmother's abandonment had shaped my mother's parenting, which had in turn shaped my attachment style and relationship patterns.

I had to acknowledge that some of my most fundamental beliefs about myself—that I'm not enough, that I'm unworthy of love, that I need to earn my right to exist—

weren't actually mine to begin with. They were handed down to me, like some toxic family legacy.

The hardest part came next: I had to begin challenging and changing these beliefs, creating new patterns, and healing not just for myself but also for the generations before me who didn't have the resources or awareness to heal themselves.

It's exhausting work, this healing business. Some days, I want to slip back into the familiar comfort of my dysfunction. At least it's known territory. At least I understand the rules there.

But then I remember that I'm not just doing this for myself. I'm doing it to break a cycle that has caused suffering for generations. I'm doing it because someone has to be the one to say, "This pattern stops with me."

The Science Behind the Madness

If you're sitting there thinking, "This sounds like a load of new-age bollocks," I get it. I was sceptical too. But the science behind intergenerational trauma is actually quite robust.

Epigenetics, the study of how behaviours and the environment can cause changes that affect how your genes work, has shown that trauma can alter gene expression. These alterations can be passed down to future generations.

A 2014 study published in Nature Neuroscience found that mice trained to fear a specific smell passed this fear down to their offspring, even though they had never encountered it before. The children and grandchildren of these mice showed the same fearful response to the scent, suggesting that the memory of the trauma was somehow encoded in their DNA.

Similar studies with humans, particularly with Holocaust survivors and their descendants, have found that children of survivors often exhibit similar stress responses to their parents, despite never having experienced the Holocaust themselves.

Dr. Rachel Yehuda, a professor of psychiatry and neuroscience, has conducted extensive research in this area. Her studies have shown that children of Holocaust survivors have lower levels of cortisol, a stress hormone, similar to their parents who experienced the trauma directly. This suggests that the biological effects of trauma can indeed be inherited.

But it's not just about biology. Trauma also gets passed down through parenting styles, family dynamics, and the stories we tell (or don't tell) about our past.

A parent who experienced neglect might become overly protective of their child, or they might repeat the pattern and neglect their child as well. A parent who never felt safe might create an environment of hypervigilance, teaching their child always to be alert for danger. A parent who was shamed might unintentionally shame their child in the same ways.

These patterns aren't passed down because parents are trying to harm their children. Quite the opposite, most parents are doing the best they can with the tools they have. But if those tools are shaped by unresolved trauma, the patterns continue.

Zelda Marsh

The Ancestral Healing Journey

So, what does healing ancestral trauma actually look like? For me, it's been a multi-faceted approach that addresses both the physical manifestations of trauma in my body and the psychological patterns in my mind.

First, there's the work of becoming aware of the patterns. This involves looking honestly at my family history, noticing the recurring themes, and connecting them to my own behaviours and beliefs. It's like being a detective in my own life, looking for clues that connect present struggles to past events.

Then there's the somatic work, healing the trauma stored in my body. This has involved various body-based therapies like somatic experiencing, EMDR (Eye Movement Desensitisation and Reprocessing), and even simple practices like yoga and mindful breathing. The goal is to release the trauma stored in my nervous system and teach my body that it's safe now.

There's also the cognitive work of challenging and changing my inherited beliefs. Traditional talk therapy, along with practices like cognitive-behavioural therapy and internal family systems work, has been helpful in this area. I've had to identify the negative beliefs I absorbed from my family system: "I'm not enough," "I'm responsible for everyone else's feelings," "It's not safe to trust", and actively work to replace them with healthier alternatives.

Perhaps most importantly, there's the relational work. Healing happens in relationships. Many of our deepest wounds occurred in relationships, and it's in relationships that they can be healed. This has meant surrounding myself with safe people who respect boundaries and can offer the secure attachment I didn't receive as a child.

It's also meant having compassion for my ancestors, understanding that they were doing their best with what they had. My grandmother wasn't deliberately trying to wound my mother; she was operating from her own unhealed trauma. My mother wasn't intentionally passing down anxious attachment; she was loving me the best way she knew how.

This compassion doesn't excuse harmful behaviour, but it does help to break the cycle of blame and shame that often accompanies family trauma. It allows me to see the humanity in my ancestors' struggles and recognise that they were wounded children once.

In her book The Choice, Dr. Edith Eva Eger, a Holocaust survivor and psychologist, discusses the importance of compassion: "Our painful experiences aren't a liability—they're a gift. They give us perspective and meaning, an opportunity to find our unique purpose and our strength."

I'm not sure I'd go as far as calling my ancestral trauma a "gift," but I do recognise that healing it has given me insights and strengths I might not have otherwise developed. It's made me more compassionate, self-aware, and committed to breaking harmful patterns.

Zelda Marsh

The Ongoing Work

Healing ancestral trauma isn't a one-and-done deal. It's not like I woke up one day and thought, "Brilliant, sorted that ancestral trauma. What's next on the to-do list?"

It's ongoing work. Some days, I catch myself falling back into old patterns—people-pleasing, abandoning myself to keep others happy, seeking validation from unavailable people. The difference now is that I recognise these patterns for what they are: echoes of ancestral wounds, not truths about who I am or what I deserve.

And on the days when the work feels too hard, when I'm tempted to give in to the familiar comfort of my dysfunction, I remind myself of what's at stake. I'm not just healing for myself; I'm healing for my ancestors who couldn't heal themselves. I'm healing for anyone who comes after me, breaking the chain so they don't have to carry what I carried.

There's a Jewish concept called "tikkun Olam," which means "repairing the world." The idea is that each of us is responsible for leaving the world better than we found it. Healing my ancestral trauma is my form of tikkun Olam. It's my way of repairing a small corner of the world, of ensuring that certain patterns of suffering end with me.

Is it easy? Not by a long shot. There are days when I'd rather blame my parents for my issues and be done with it. There are days when the weight of generations of trauma feels too heavy to bear.

But then I remember something my therapist told me: "Healing happens in spirals, not straight lines." We revisit the same wounds at deeper levels, gaining new insights and releasing old patterns bit by bit. It's not about reaching some perfect state of healing; it's about continuing to show up for the process, day after day.

Sometimes, in quiet moments, I feel a sense of connection to the women who came before me—my mother, grandmother, and great-grandmother. I feel their struggles and strengths. I feel their hope that someday, someone in the family line will break free from the patterns that bound them.

I whisper to them in those moments, "I'm doing it. I'm breaking the cycle. This healing is for all of us."

And somewhere, in whatever realm ancestors reside, I like to think they're cheering me on.

The Northern Resilience

I've come to appreciate one more thing about ancestral patterns: we also inherit resilience alongside the trauma. The same ancestors who passed down their wounds also passed down their strength, survival skills, and ability to endure.

My Northern English heritage isn't just about stoicism and emotional repression. It's also about grit, humour in the face of adversity, and a stubborn refusal to be defeated by circumstances.

My grandmother lived through World War II, raised children in poverty, and still managed to find joy in simple pleasures. My mother navigated a difficult marriage, financial struggles, and her own unresolved trauma, yet still showed up for me with love and did her best to give me a better life than she had.

Zelda Marsh

These women weren't just carriers of trauma; they were also carriers of incredible strength. And that strength is as much a part of my inheritance as the wounds.

Dr. Boris Cyrulnik, a neurologist and psychologist who survived the Holocaust as a child, developed the concept of "resilience" in psychology. He defines it as "the capacity to develop positively, in a socially acceptable way, despite stress or adversity that normally involves the risk of a negative outcome."

In other words, resilience is the ability to bounce back from adversity and find ways to thrive despite difficult circumstances. This resilience can also be passed down through generations.

So yes, I inherited trauma patterns from my ancestors. But I also inherited their resilience, survival skills, and capacity to endure and even find moments of joy amid struggles.

My Northern English heritage gave me not just a talent for emotional repression and a fondness for tea as a solution to all problems, but also a dry sense of humour that helps me cope with life's absurdities, a practical approach to challenges, and a deep well of strength to draw from when things get tough.

As I work to heal ancestral wounds, I also honour ancestral strengths. I recognise that both are part of my inheritance and have shaped who I am.

In the end, healing ancestral trauma isn't about rejecting my heritage or blaming my ancestors. It's about consciously choosing which parts of that heritage to carry forward and which parts to leave behind. It's about honouring the full complexity of where I come from while creating a new path forward.

And sometimes, it's about raising a cup of tea to those who came before me—acknowledging both their wounds and their wisdom, struggles and strength—and saying, "I see you. I honour you. And I'm doing the healing work that perhaps you couldn't do."

That's not just healing; that's ancestral justice. And it tastes much better than bitterness, even if it requires swallowing some uncomfortable truths along with my Yorkshire Tea and a Rich tea biscuit.

PART TWO: THE BODY KEEPS SCORE

How trauma manifests physically and shapes our relationships

Chapter 5: The Body's Ledger

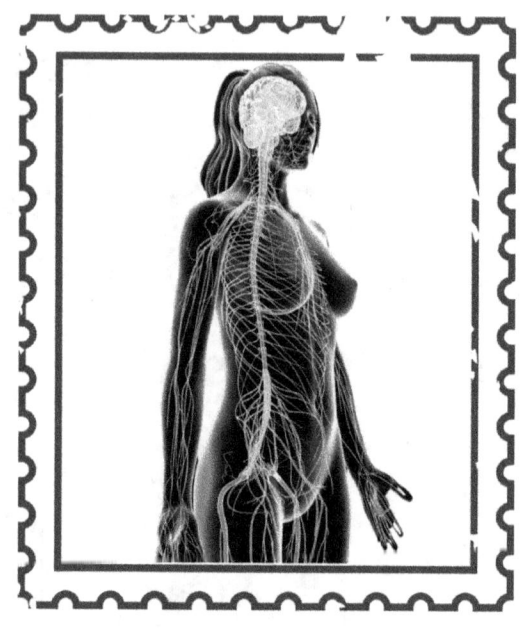

Zelda Marsh

The Nervous System's Perfect Memory

Let's get one thing straight, love—your body is not just some meat suit you're dragging around. She's a whole effing library of everything you've ever been through. Every time someone hurt you, ignored you, or made you shrink? Yeah, she logged it.

For years, I thought I was just "sensitive." I couldn't handle a raised voice, got jumpy when someone slammed a door and had a stomach that tied itself in knots over nothing.

Except it wasn't nothing.

It was everything.

Your nervous system doesn't forget a bloody thing, that's what makes it both brilliant and brutal. While your conscious mind might say, "That was ages ago; get over it," your body's keeping a detailed ledger of every slight, every scare, and every moment you felt unsafe.

Dr. Stephen Porges calls this the Polyvagal Theory: a fancy name for how your nervous system decides whether you're safe or in danger. According to him, we have three primary states: social engagement (when we feel safe and connected), mobilisation (fight or flight), and immobilisation (freeze or collapse).

The kicker? This system operates below conscious awareness. You don't decide to have a panic attack in Tesco because someone dropped a tin; your nervous system makes that call before you've even registered what the noise was.

I Don't Need Your Forgiveness To Heal

It turns out that your nervous system can't tell the difference between your dad shouting in 1995 and your boss sending a blunt email in 2023. It just goes: *Danger!*

And boom: your heart's racing, you've lost your appetite, and you're crying in the toilet like you've just been dumped. Again.

That's what Dr. Gabor Maté calls "trauma imprinting." It's your past stuck on repeat in your body.

And here's where Bessel van der Kolk comes in again, **The Body Keeps the Score**. That title hit me like a slap. Because it's not just a book, it's a bloody diagnosis.

It's why your back seizes up before family Christmas. It's also why your shoulders feel like concrete every Monday. And why does your gut act like it's running from a sabre-toothed tiger when you're just standing in Tesco?

It's not your fault, love. It's your body doing what it has to do to survive.

Zelda Marsh

The Physical Symptoms Nobody Connects

Let me tell you about my body's ledger, which I carried for decades without understanding what I was reading.

I had migraines that would knock me sideways, always around birthdays or holidays. I had IBS that flared up before any confrontation. I had eczema that bloomed across my hands whenever I felt trapped. I had insomnia that kept me wired and exhausted, especially when things were actually going well in my life.

For years, doctors gave me creams, pills, diets, and that special look that says, "It's probably just stress, love." It is as if "just stress" isn't your entire nervous system screaming for help.

What they didn't tell me, what nobody bloody told me, was that these weren't random ailments. They were my body's desperate attempts to communicate what my mouth couldn't say.

According to Dr. Bessel van der Kolk, trauma survivors often develop what he calls "somatic symptoms"—physical manifestations of emotional distress. It's like your body's speaking in code, and unless you know the cypher, you're left thinking you're just unlucky with your health.

My migraines? They weren't random. They happened when I felt pressured to perform happiness during historically unsafe or disappointing times. My body was saying, "Last time we celebrated your birthday, your mum got drunk and ruined it. Let's shut down before that happens again."

The IBS? Classic fight-or-flight response in the gut. When stressed, blood diverts away from digestion to our limbs (so we can run or fight). Do that chronically, and you have a digestive system as reliable as a chocolate fireguard.

The eczema on my hands? Dr Gabor Maté would point out that skin conditions often flare up in people who feel they need to "break out" of something but can't. My hands were literally trying to shed the skin I was living in.

And the insomnia when things were going well? That's the nervous system saying, "This feels unfamiliar. Unfamiliar equals potentially dangerous. Stay alert!"

It's not hypochondria. It's not a weakness. It's not "all in your head."

It's in your body. And your body never lies.

The Amygdala: Your Inner Drama Queen

Let's discuss this little almond-shaped drama queen in your brain—the amygdala. Its job? To keep you alive by constantly scanning for danger.

In a healthy, non-traumatised nervous system, the amygdala works with the prefrontal cortex (the rational thinking part of your brain) to assess threats accurately. "Is that rustling in the bushes a tiger or just the wind? Let me check before I freak out."

But trauma rewires this system. Studies using FMRI (Functional Magnetic Resonance Imaging) scans show that in people with PTSD or chronic trauma, the amygdala becomes hyperactive while the prefrontal cortex shows reduced activity. In plain English? Your alarm system gets louder while your rational thinking gets quieter.

This explains why I'd have full-blown panic responses to minor triggers—a certain tone of voice, a door slamming, or even a particular smell could send me spiralling. My amygdala screamed, "DANGER!" before my prefrontal cortex could say, "Hang on, let's think about this."

It also explains why logical thinking rarely helps with trauma responses. Telling yourself, "I'm being irrational", doesn't work when the irrational part of your brain is running the show.

This isn't a character flaw. It's neurobiology. Your experiences have literally shaped your brain.

The Vagus Nerve: Your Body's Information Highway

If you want to understand how trauma lives in the body, you've got to meet the vagus nerve: the longest cranial nerve in your body, running from your brain stem down through your chest and into your gut.

Think of it as the information superhighway between your brain and your body. It carries messages both ways, meaning your gut feelings are real neurological events, not just metaphors.

Dr. Stephen Porges, who developed the Polyvagal Theory, explains that the vagus nerve has two branches: the ventral (front) and dorsal (back). The ventral branch helps us feel safe and connected. The dorsal branch activates when we're in extreme danger, causing us to freeze or collapse.

In trauma survivors, this system gets dysregulated. We might get stuck in dorsal vagal responses (feeling numb, disconnected, exhausted) or sympathetic arousal (anxiety, panic, rage) without the ability to access that ventral vagal state of safety.

This explained so much about my own experiences—why I could swing from hyperactive anxiety to complete emotional shutdown, sometimes within the same day. Why could I be laughing one minute and dissociating the next? My vagal system was like a faulty light switch, flipping between states without my conscious control.

Understanding this was revolutionary. It meant I wasn't crazy, weak, or "too sensitive." My nervous system was doing exactly what it had learned to do to keep me alive in unsafe circumstances.

The problem wasn't my responses; it was that these responses were happening in situations where they weren't needed anymore.

Hypervigilance: The Exhausting Superpower

Let's talk about hypervigilance, that constant state of scanning for danger that trauma survivors know all too well.

From the outside, it might look like paranoia or anxiety. But from the inside? It's exhausting vigilance. Always watching and always listening. Always ready.

I could walk into a room and instantly know who was in a bad mood, who had been arguing, and who was safe to talk to. I could hear a slight change in someone's breathing pattern and knew they were upset before they did. I could feel tension building before an argument erupted.

This wasn't magic. It was survival.

In her groundbreaking work on trauma, Dr. Judith Herman explains that hypervigilance develops as an adaptive response to unpredictable danger. If you grow up never knowing when the next blow (physical or emotional) will come, your nervous system adapts by staying on high alert all the time.

The cost? Exhaustion. Chronic stress. A nervous system that never fully relaxes.

The benefit? An almost supernatural ability to read people and situations. An intuition so finely tuned it borders on psychic.

Because of their heightened perceptive abilities, many trauma survivors become exceptional at caring professions, creative fields, or crisis management. Our wounds become our gifts if we learn to work with them rather than against them.

But first, we have to recognise that hypervigilance, while useful in certain contexts, isn't a sustainable way to live. It's like running your car engine at full throttle 24/7. Eventually, something's going to burn out.

The Immune System: Your Body's Boundary Keeper

Here's something they don't tell you about trauma: it doesn't just mess with your mind and your nerves—it compromises your immune system too.

Research shows that chronic stress and trauma can actually suppress immune function, making you more vulnerable to everything from common colds to autoimmune conditions.

Dr. Gabor Maté, in his book "When the Body Says No," explains how emotional stress, particularly the stress of maintaining a façade while suppressing true feelings, can contribute to physical illness. The energy required to keep pushing down pain and to keep functioning despite internal chaos takes a massive toll on the body's resources.

This explained why I was always catching every bug going around. Why did I develop mysterious rashes, unexplained pain, and chronic fatigue? My immune system was too busy dealing with the internal threat of unprocessed trauma to fight external threats effectively.

It also explained the timing of my illnesses, how I'd often get sick right after a crisis had passed, not during it. In survival mode, my body would pump out enough stress hormones to keep me functioning. But the moment I relaxed? Crash. My system would collapse under the weight of what it had been carrying.

This isn't psychosomatic in the dismissive sense that doctors sometimes use. It's the very real physical consequence of a body that's been in danger mode for too long.

The Gut: Your Second Brain

Did you know you've got a second brain? It's true. Your gut contains more neurons than a cat's entire brain. Scientists call it the enteric nervous system, which communicates directly with your central brain through the vagus nerve.

This explains why anxiety feels like butterflies in your stomach, why grief makes you lose your appetite. Why fear can give you diarrhoea. Your gut isn't just responding to your emotions; it's helping to create them.

For trauma survivors, gut issues are incredibly common. IBS, food sensitivities, and chronic indigestion aren't just annoying health problems. They're often direct manifestations of a nervous system stuck in fight-or-flight.

When you're in danger, your body diverts blood away from digestion (you don't need to digest that sandwich when you're running from a tiger). Do this chronically, and your digestive system becomes compromised.

Add to this that 90% of your serotonin (the "happy hormone") is produced in your gut, and you start to see why emotional and digestive health are so intertwined.

My own gut issues began in childhood and followed me into adulthood, bloating, pain, unpredictable bowels that the slightest stress could trigger. For years, I tried elimination diets, probiotics, and medications. Some helped a bit, but nothing resolved the underlying issue.

Because the underlying issue wasn't in my gut, it was in my nervous system. My gut was just the messenger, trying desperately to tell me something wasn't right.

When I finally started addressing the trauma directly, my digestive issues didn't disappear overnight, but they became manageable in a way they never had been before. As my nervous system began to regulate, my gut started to heal.

The Body's Timeline: Why You Feel It Now

One of the most confusing aspects of trauma is its timeline. Why do symptoms often appear years or even decades after the traumatic events? Why might you function relatively well through the actual trauma, only to fall apart when you're finally safe?

Dr. Peter Levine explains this through what he calls the "discharge" process. In nature, animals naturally discharge trauma energy after a threatening event—they shake, tremble, and then return to normal. Humans, with our complex brains and social conditioning, often interrupt this natural process. We're told to "be strong," to "get over it," to "move on."

So, instead of discharging, we contain, hold, and freeze the energy of the trauma in our bodies.

It stays there—sometimes for years—until something triggers its release or until the containment system can no longer contain it.

This explained why, in my thirties, I suddenly started having panic attacks related to childhood events. Why did certain physical symptoms appear seemingly out of nowhere? My body wasn't creating new problems—it was finally revealing old ones that had been there all along.

It's like those videos where they drain a swamp and suddenly find all sorts of things hidden under the water. The objects were always there—they just couldn't be seen until the conditions changed.

Safety, ironically, is often when trauma symptoms emerge most strongly. Only when we're safe can our nervous system finally afford to process what happened.

Reflection: Listening to Your Body's Wisdom

The most profound shift in my healing journey came when I stopped fighting my body and started listening to it.

What if those migraines weren't inconveniences but messages? What if that chronic pain wasn't just bad luck but information? What if my body wasn't broken but communicating in the only language it knew?

This doesn't mean the symptoms aren't real or that they don't need practical management. But it does mean that treating only the symptom without addressing their roots is like putting a plaster on a splinter without removing it first.

Your body keeps the score but also holds the key to healing. Every symptom is a doorway. Every pain contains information. Every reaction, however uncomfortable, is trying to tell you something important.

The question isn't, "How do I stop this?" but "What is this trying to tell me?"

When we start asking that question, with curiosity rather than judgment, compassion rather than frustration, we begin the real work of healing.

Not by silencing the body, but by finally learning its language.

I Don't Need Your Forgiveness To Heal

Reflection Prompt: What physical symptoms have been recurring in your life? If these symptoms could speak, what might they be trying to tell you? Place a hand on the part of your body that troubles you most and ask, "What do you need me to know?" Then, sit quietly and see what arises.

Zelda Marsh

Chapter 6: Relationships as Mirrors

First Husband: Trauma Magnetism Dressed Up as Fate

Relationships. The bloody battlefield where all your unhealed trauma comes out to play. Where your body remembers what your mind tries to forget. Where your nervous system gets to say, "I told you so" over and over again.

Let me take you through my own relationship car crashes, not for the drama, but because I bet my bottom quid, or dollar now, you'll see yourself in at least one of them. And maybe, just maybe, you'll understand why your body's been trying to warn you all along. Husband number one. Love at first sight, was it trauma magnetism dressed up as fate? Either way, we met, merged, and made a family.

He was the youngest child in a stable, loving family, the only boy handed everything on a silver platter. Friends galore, I had no clue what it meant to **need** anything. When we met, it was fireworks—first sight—full heart. And at first, he made me feel safe, like **finally**, I was the chosen one.

But slowly, that safety turned into shackles. Possessiveness crept in like mould; it was quiet, spreading, and toxic. He didn't understand why I needed space **and** closeness. He couldn't grasp the emotional weather patterns I lived with daily.

Before I knew it, I wasn't in a partnership; I was a prized possession with a changing mat and three kids under five.

No one, and I mean no one, gets to own me. **Or so I thought.**

The Attachment Dance: Why We Choose What Feels Familiar

Here's what the fancy attachment theorists would tell you: we're drawn to what feels familiar, not what feels good. And when you've grown up with inconsistent love, with abandonment, with emotional whiplash, guess what feels familiar? *Hint: it's not stable, secure relationships.*

Dr. Amir Levine, who wrote "Attached," explains that we develop attachment styles in childhood that play out in adult relationships. If you had inconsistent caregiving (hello, mum who left and dad who was emotionally unavailable), you're likely to develop what's called an "anxious attachment style."

People with anxious attachments crave closeness but fear abandonment. We're hypervigilant to signs of rejection. We often choose partners who are emotionally unavailable because the push-pull dynamic feels like home.

And that's exactly what I did. I chose a man who made me work for love, kept me slightly off-balance, and could be warm one day and cold the next. Not because I wanted to suffer, but because my nervous system recognised the pattern. "Ah," it said, "this feels like childhood. I know how to navigate this."

The problem? What's familiar isn't always what's healthy.

My body knew this relationship wasn't right long before my mind caught up. The constant knot in my stomach, the tension headaches, the insomnia, the way my shoulders lived somewhere around my ears, these weren't just stress symptoms; they were my body's early warning system trying desperately to get my attention.

But I ignored it. Because the alternative, being alone, starting over, admitting I'd made a mistake, felt even more threatening to my trauma-wired brain.

Parenting While Triggered: The Greatest Challenge

Post-divorce, three kids in tow, I played the ultimate game of Guess Who?, only with bills, school runs, and therapy worksheets instead of bubble baths and gin nights.

I bought a house on my own. Me. A woman who once flinched when signing a lease now held the keys to a future; I was determined to make it different. I built a support network from scratch, coffee chats at school gates, borrowed casseroles from kind neighbours, and therapy groups that cracked me open and stitched me back up.

I did my best to parent differently from **her,** the mother who loved with conditions and never learned softness. I even stopped drinking boxed wine, well, mostly. And while everyone else posted picture-perfect family snaps, I juggled nappies and notes from school while whispering mantras to myself in the loo.

I moved near her again, thinking things could heal; we could start over. Brave or bonkers? A bit of both. But it was growth, growth wrapped in thorns, but growth nonetheless.

I sometimes caught myself sounding like her—barking orders through gritted teeth, flaring with stress that didn't belong to the moment. And when I did, I'd sit in my car, hands clenched around the steering wheel, whispering, "You're not her. You're breaking the pattern."

Because I didn't just want to be different, I wanted to be free.

The Neuroscience of Parenting with Trauma

Parenting when you've got trauma is like trying to defuse a bomb while someone keeps shouting at you and throwing glitter in your face. It's intense, it's messy, and one wrong move feels catastrophic.

Dr. Daniel Siegel, a clinical professor of psychiatry, talks about "flipping your lid." Imagine your brain has two parts: the upstairs brain (rational, thoughtful) and the downstairs brain (emotional, reactive). When you're triggered, you "flip your lid", your upstairs brain goes offline, and your downstairs brain takes over.

This happens to everyone sometimes. But for trauma survivors? It happens faster, more intensely, and with less warning.

A child's tantrum isn't just annoying; it can catapult you back to feeling powerless, rejected, or threatened. Their normal developmental behaviours can trigger your deepest wounds. Their needs can activate your primal fears of not being enough.

And here's the cruel irony: the very moments when our children need us to be most regulated are often the moments when our own trauma gets triggered.

I remember standing in the kitchen, my youngest having an epic meltdown over something trivial. I felt it happening, the tightness in my chest, the ringing in my ears, the overwhelming urge to either scream or shut down completely. My body was going into fight-flight-freeze, not because there was actual danger, but because the noise, the chaos, and the feeling of not being able to fix it were activating old neural pathways.

At that moment, I wasn't responding to my child. I was responding to my past.

The difference between repeating and breaking patterns often comes down to this: can you recognise when you're triggered? Can you pause before you react? Can you soothe your nervous system enough to respond to what's happening now, not what happened then?

It's not about being perfect. It's about being aware. Sometimes, awareness means sitting on the kitchen floor, breathing through the trigger, and showing your children that emotions aren't emergencies; they're information.

Husband Number Two: Spiritual Bypassing in Human Form

By this time, I was in full witchy wellness mode. I was taking holistic healing courses, obtaining massage qualifications, having salt lamps in every room, moon-bathing, and performing chakra cleanses. I also had crystals stuffed down my bra like spiritual armour.

Zelda Marsh

Husband Number Two came along like a spiritual saviour. He ticked all the boxes—mindfulness, mantras, even knew what a moon cycle was (or pretended to). On paper, it looked like a cosmic match. But being spiritually aligned doesn't always mean being emotionally mature.

I was doing the work, shadow diving, crying on yoga mats, writing trauma letters to my inner child, while he… sat in front of the telly, eating cheese toasties and calling me dramatic.

The more I healed, the more he resisted. My vibration rose, and his resentment deepened. I saw the possibility, and he saw a problem. And then came the betrayals.

He cheated. Then cheated again. And again. Honestly, the man was so predictable he could've been a horoscope. Every time I found out, he gaslit me. Said I was paranoid. Too intense. Too much.

So, I worked harder to be lovable and tried to be softer, quieter, sparklier, and brighter. But that's the twisted alchemy of trauma, you start confusing silence for stability.

Spoiler: it still wasn't enough for him. But that wasn't about me.

It took a long time to realise that the love I was giving him was the love I needed to give myself.

The Trauma Bond: When Pain Feels Like Love

What I didn't understand then, but research makes painfully clear now, is that I was caught in what psychologists call a "trauma bond." It's a powerful emotional attachment formed through cycles of abuse, betrayal, and intermittent reinforcement.

Dr. Patrick Carnes, who coined the term, explains that trauma bonds form when a person experiencing abuse also experiences positive feelings from their abuser. The unpredictability creates a biochemical addiction, literally. Your brain gets flooded with stress chemicals during the bad times, then dopamine and oxytocin during the good times. This roller coaster creates a dependency more potent than many drug addictions.

That's why leaving an abusive relationship isn't just emotionally challenging, it's physically painful. Your body goes through actual withdrawal.

With my second husband, the pattern was textbook. He'd cheat, I'd discover it, deny it, I'd find proof, break down and promise to change. There'd be a honeymoon period of intense connection, and the cycle would start again.

Each time, my body tried to warn me. Insomnia before I found evidence. He had mysterious rashes when he was being particularly manipulative. Gut problems that flared up when he was lying to my face. My body knew the truth before my mind would accept it.

But I ignored these signals because the alternative, facing betrayal, the failure of another marriage, and the shame of having "chosen wrong" again, felt even more threatening.

This isn't a weakness. It's neurobiology. Trauma bonds hijack the same brain systems involved in addiction. They're not a choice, they're a trap.

Zelda Marsh

The Tick Box Man from Hell: When Red Flags Look Like Home

Post-divorce/Relationships (again), I went seeking love with a cocktail of trauma and hope. In walked Mr. Tall, Dark & Dangerously Delusional. A walking spiritual test sent by the Universe to say, "Still got lessons to learn, babe?"

He was charming. Magnetic. The kind of man who said all the right things with just enough intensity to make you mistake passion and obsession. He looked the part. Talked the talk. Love-bombed me like a bloody fireworks display. And I: still healing, raw, hoping, and fell for the fantasy.

He knew what to say and when to say it. He mirrored all the parts of me I was finally starting to like. It felt like chemistry. In reality, it was chaos. There were red flags. There were beige flags. Hell, there were flaming banners of warning flying through the air, and I ignored them all because I was starving for something that felt like a connection.

And then came the truth. The drugs. The manipulation. The slow, creeping control. His idea of love wasn't love. It was ownership. It was power. It was punishment for daring to rise too far beyond what he could contain.

Violence disguised as passion. Apologies that never stuck. I almost lost everything, including myself.

That wasn't just heartbreak. That wasn't just trauma.

That was bedrock. And not the rose quartz kind, either. It was jagged, black, and volcanic. The type of rock bottom that burns on the way down and takes years to claw your way back up from.

But claw, I did.

The Body During Domestic Violence: Fight, Flight, Freeze, and Fawn

What happens to your body during domestic violence isn't just emotional damage: it's neurobiological rewiring. And understanding this is crucial for healing.

Dr Bessel van der Kolk explains that in situations of inescapable threat (like being in a violent relationship), the body cycles through survival responses: fight, flight, freeze, and fawn.

Fight: The surge of adrenaline, the racing heart, the clenched fists. Flight: The desperate need to escape, to run, to hide. Freeze: When neither fighting nor fleeing seems possible, the body immobilises you, goes numb, disconnected, shut down. Fawn: The survival response least talked about but incredibly common in abuse—you try to please the abuser, to become what they want, to make yourself smaller and less threatening.

I cycled through all of these. Sometimes within the same hour. My body was desperately trying every strategy it knew to keep me alive.

The Hypervigilance is always watching for signs of his mood changing. The stomach problems were caused by my digestion shutting down because my body was constantly in danger mode. The dissociation of floating above myself during the worst moments, as if I weren't there. The people-pleasing: becoming smaller, quieter, and more compliant to avoid triggering his rage.

These weren't character flaws or weaknesses. They were survival mechanisms. My body was doing exactly what it was designed to do in the face of a threat.

The problem came after I left. Because these responses, which were adaptive in danger, became maladaptive in safety. My body was still responding as if I were in constant threat, even when I wasn't.

This explains the panic attacks that came months after leaving. The nightmares. The startle at loud noises. The difficulty in trusting new people. My body was still operating on the old programming.

Understanding this was the first step toward reprogramming it.

The Healing Relationship: What Safety Actually Feels Like

After the Tick Box Man from Hell, I did something radical: I stayed single. Not just for a few months. For years.

Not because I was afraid of relationships (though, fair play, I was), but because I needed to learn what safety felt like. In my own company. In my own skin. In my own nervous system.

This was when I discovered something shocking: safety often feels boring at first. When your nervous system is used to chaos, calm can feel underwhelming. Stability can feel flat when you're accustomed to the highs and lows of trauma bonds.

Dr. Judith Herman talks about this in her work on complex trauma. She explains that trauma survivors often mistake intensity for intimacy. We confuse drama with passion. We're so used to relationships that keep us on edge that anything else feels... wrong.

This explained why I'd always been drawn to complicated men, why "nice guys" seemed boring, and why stability made me itchy. My nervous system was calibrated for chaos, and safety felt like a foreign language.

Learning to recalibrate took time. It meant sitting with the discomfort of calm, recognising when I was creating drama because the peace felt too threatening, and understanding that the butterflies I'd always associated with attraction were actually anxiety, my body's warning system, not a sign of love.

Gradually, my definition of attraction changed. I started to find peace attractive, consistency attractive, and emotional availability attractive. Not because these things were exciting, but because they finally allowed my nervous system to relax.

And when I eventually did enter a new relationship, it was with someone who understood trauma. Who didn't take my triggers personally? Who gave me space to heal without trying to fix me? Who recognised that my reactions weren't about him, sometimes they were echoes of old wounds.

That's what a healing relationship looks like. It's not perfect, not without challenges, but fundamentally safe. It's a container where both people can be human, make mistakes, trigger each other, and repair. The goal isn't to avoid all conflict but to navigate it in ways that don't re-traumatise.

Zelda Marsh

Reflection: Your Body in Relationships

Think about your most significant romantic, familial, and friendship relationships. How does your body feel in each of them?

Do you tense up before seeing certain people? Do you exhale fully in their presence or hold your breath? Do you sleep well after spending time with them, or lie awake replaying interactions?

Your body knows who's safe and who isn't long before your mind is willing to admit it.

The next time you're with someone important to you, try this: Close your eyes for a moment and scan your body from head to toe. Notice any areas of tension, constriction, or discomfort. Also, notice any areas of warmth, expansion, or ease.

This isn't about judging the relationship; it's about gathering information. Your body constantly gives you data about your environment, including its people. Learning to read this data is one of the most powerful tools for healing.

Ultimately, healthy relationships aren't just about who the other person is but about how your nervous system responds to them. And that response isn't just emotional—it's physical, visceral, and profoundly honest.

Your body doesn't lie about relationships. It's time to start listening.

I Don't Need Your Forgiveness To Heal

Reflection Prompt: Think of a relationship that feels challenging. Where in your body do you feel tension when you think about this person? Now, think of someone who feels safe. How does your body respond differently? What might these physical responses be trying to tell you about these relationships?

Zelda Marsh

Chapter 7: The Masks We Wear

The Comedy of Survival

I wasn't the class clown, not really. That title never quite fit. I wasn't the one jumping on tables or cracking jokes to get attention. I was more strategic than that. I was the queen of distraction. The sly architect of the perfect wisecrack, the jaw-dropping story, the sarcastic twist that left people unsure if it was stand-up or soul-bleed. I'd reel them in with wit, leave them laughing-or stunned and vanish behind the performance.

People saw the confident, funny, take-no-prisoners gal. The one who'd have you cackling over coffee and simultaneously solving your existential crisis. What didn't they see? The girl is crying over the Cornflakes ads. The woman sobbing at X Factor auditions like she raised those singers. (It didn't matter if they were tone-deaf—I felt it all.)

I've cried over books, fridge adverts, the smell of someone's perfume, and songs that triggered memories I thought I'd buried under years of bravado. But the biggest culprits? Netflix series. It doesn't even matter what the storyline is, happy families, deep trauma arcs, or even a heartwarming reunion episode. I'm sobbing like a cracked kettle. I'm not built for surface-level anything. If you bring me vibes, I'm bringing tissues, trauma, and the emotional capacity of a Greek chorus. I don't just feel your energy; I inhale it, sob it out, and then spend the rest of the night wondering why I'm wrung out like a wet sponge from just walking into a tense room.

The Science of Emotional Armour

You know that phrase, "I'm fine?" It's British for "I'm falling apart but trying not to be an inconvenience." I used it daily, weekly, and on a loop. I said it while I was drowning in grief, whispering it while I was shoving down the sob that had camped in my chest for years. "I'm fine" was code for "don't look too closely."

Robin Williams once said, "I think the saddest people always try their hardest to make people happy... Because they know what it feels like to feel absolutely worthless, and they don't want anybody else to feel like that." And I felt that in my bones. I **was** that. The entertainer. The emotional caretaker. The tragic clown in a sparkly headwrap.

And look where that humour got him. The man who made the whole world laugh, who tricked us into thinking he lived in a constant state of joy, until it heartbreakingly turned out he didn't. His world wasn't the oyster we thought it was. It was an ocean of silent suffering dressed up in punchlines. And just like that, it became terrifyingly clear: even the brightest laugh can hide the darkest ache.

But what happens in the body when we use humour as a shield? According to Dr Peter Levine, creator of Somatic Experiencing therapy, it's a sophisticated form of dissociation that disconnects from overwhelming emotions by redirecting attention.

When trauma threatens to overwhelm us, the nervous system has several options: fight, flight, freeze, or, in this case, a variation of the "fawn" response, which uses charm, humour, and people-pleasing to create safety.

The body literally shifts its physiological state. Heart rate changes, breathing patterns alter, and facial muscles engage differently. It's not just a psychological strategy; it's a full-body adaptation.

And it works. Humour is an effective short-term strategy for managing unbearable feelings. It creates a social connection, diffuses tension, and gives a momentary sense of control when we feel powerless.

The problem comes when it's our only strategy, when we can't turn it off, use it to avoid rather than process, or when the mask becomes so comfortable that we forget there's a face underneath.

The Empath's Curse: Feeling Everything

Let's talk about being an empath: not the woo-woo "I can read your aura" kind (though maybe that too), but the "I literally feel your feelings in my body" kind.

For years, I thought I was just "too sensitive." There's actually neuroscience behind this. Dr. Elaine Aron's research on Highly Sensitive Persons (HSPS) shows that about 20% of the population has a nervous system that processes sensory information more deeply than others. We notice more, feel more and get overwhelmed more easily.

Add trauma to this natural sensitivity, and you've got a perfect storm because trauma makes the nervous system even more reactive, vigilant, and tuned into subtle cues of danger or distress.

I could walk into a room and instantly absorb the emotional temperature. Someone angry? My stomach would knot. Someone sad? My chest would tighten. Someone anxious? My breathing would be shallow. It wasn't empathy in the "I understand how you feel" sense; it was embodied empathy. I was literally taking on other people's emotional states.

Zelda Marsh

This isn't mystical; it's neurological. It's mirror neurons and limbic resonance. It's a nervous system so attuned to others that it forgets to maintain its boundaries.

The cost? Exhaustion, confusion about which feelings were actually mine, a sense of responsibility for everyone else's emotional well-being, and a profound difficulty distinguishing between empathy and enmeshment.

I'd leave social gatherings drained, not because I'm an introvert (though I am), but because I'd spent the entire time unconsciously processing everyone else's emotional baggage along with my own. It was like being a sponge that couldn't stop absorbing, even when already saturated.

Learning to be an empath with boundaries, to feel without absorbing, to care without carrying, has been one of the most challenging aspects of my healing journey. The ability to deeply feel isn't the problem; it's a gift. The problem is not knowing where I end and where others begin.

The Physical Toll of Emotional Performance

Maintaining a mask is exhausting physical labour. It's not just mentally draining; it creates actual tension in the body.

Think about what happens when you force a smile when you're sad or angry. Your facial muscles contract in an unnatural pattern. Your breathing becomes shallow. Your shoulders might rise toward your ears. Your jaw clenches. Your throat tightens to hold back what you really want to say.

Now, imagine maintaining that state for hours, days, or years. Chronic tension becomes your new normal. You forget what it feels like to be relaxed, authentic, and present in your body.

This explains the migraines that would hit me after social events where I'd been "on." It also explains the jaw pain from years of smiling through gritted teeth, the chronic throat issues from swallowing words I couldn't say, and the digestive problems from literally "stomaching" emotions that were too dangerous to express.

Dr. Gabor Maté discusses this in his work on the connection between emotional repression and physical illness. The body pays the price when we consistently suppress our authentic emotional responses. The energy required to maintain incongruence to present one face to the world while experiencing something entirely different inside creates a state of chronic stress.

Chronic stress, as we now know, is at the root of many physical illnesses. From autoimmune conditions to cancer, from heart disease to chronic fatigue, the body eventually rebels against the demand to be something it's not.

My own body rebelled in classic ways: immune system dysfunction, chronic fatigue, mysterious pain that moved around like an unwelcome houseguest. For years, doctors suggested it was "just stress" or, worse, implied it was psychosomatic in the dismissive sense.

What they didn't understand, what I didn't understand, was that it wasn't "all in my head." It was in my tissues, my cells, my nervous system. It was the physical manifestation of years of emotional labour, of maintaining a mask so convincing that even I sometimes forgot it wasn't my real face.

The Freeze Response: When Laughter Hides Shutdown

One of the least understood trauma responses is the freeze state, when the nervous system decides that neither fighting nor fleeing is possible and immobilises instead.

In humans, freeze doesn't always look like playing dead. Sometimes, it seems like laughter. Sometimes, it looks like excessive talking. Sometimes, it seems like being the life of the party while feeling completely disconnected from your body.

Dr. Stephen Porges, developer of the Polyvagal Theory, explains that the body is in a complex neurophysiological condition in freeze states. The sympathetic nervous system (fight/flight) might still be partially activated, creating a sense of internal agitation, while the dorsal vagal system creates immobilisation. The result? A person who appears animated on the outside but feels numb or disconnected on the inside.

This explained so much about my own experience how I could make a room full of people laugh while feeling like I was watching myself from a distance, how I could be articulate, funny, and engaged in conversation while feeling completely empty inside, how I could remember the words I said but not the feeling of telling them.

It wasn't acting, exactly. It was dissociation, a splitting of consciousness when the present moment is too overwhelming to inhabit fully.

And like all trauma responses, it served a purpose. It kept me functioning when falling apart wasn't an option. It maintained social connections when isolation would have been dangerous. It gave me a sense of control when everything else felt chaotic.

The problem came when it became my default state when I couldn't turn it off, when I was dissociated, even in situations that were actually safe, when I no longer knew how to be present in my own life.

The Highly Sensitive Person in a Desensitised World

Being highly sensitive in a world that values toughness is like being a houseplant in a hurricane. Everything's too loud, too bright, too fast, too much, and you're expected to tolerate and thrive in it.

Dr. Elaine Aron's research shows that high sensitivity is a genetic trait in about 20% of the population. It's not a disorder or a weakness; it's a different way of processing sensory information. HSPS have more active mirror neurons (the cells responsible for empathy), process information more deeply, and are more affected by stimuli others might not notice.

When you combine this natural sensitivity with trauma, you get someone who's not just picking up more information than others; they're also interpreting more of it as potentially threatening.

This explained why I found certain environments unbearable that others seemed to enjoy, why loud restaurants left me exhausted, why I needed so much alone time to recover from social interactions, and why certain sounds, smells, or textures could trigger a full-body stress response.

It wasn't weakness or being "too sensitive" in the pejorative sense. My nervous system was doing exactly what it was designed to do, just with the volume turned up to eleven.

Learning to honour this sensitivity rather than fight it has been transformative. Instead of pushing myself to tolerate overwhelming environments, I now recognise that my sensitivity is actually valuable information. It's telling me what my system can and cannot process effectively.

This doesn't mean avoiding life. It means making conscious choices about environments, relationships, and stimuli. It means creating buffers and boundaries. It means recognising that my need for quiet, nature, and gentleness isn't a character flaw; it's a legitimate neurological requirement.

Perhaps most importantly, it means understanding that sensitivity and strength aren't opposites. They're companions. My sensitivity makes me perceptive, empathetic, and creative. My strength allows me to honour that sensitivity in a world that often doesn't understand it.

The Body's Truth: When the Mask Slips

No matter how convincing the mask is, the body always eventually tells the truth. It might be a panic attack in the supermarket, a mysterious illness that forces you to stop, or a moment of unexpected tears when someone shows you simple kindness.

The body keeps the score, and eventually, it demands to be heard.

For me, the mask began to slip in my late thirties. I'd be in the middle of a performance, making people laugh, solving problems, being the strong one, and suddenly feel like I couldn't breathe. My vision would tunnel, my heart would race, and my hands would go numb.

The first time it happened, I thought I was having a heart attack. The second time, I wondered if I was losing my mind. By the third time, I had to face the truth: my body was staging a rebellion against decades of pretending.

These weren't just panic attacks, though; that's what doctors called them. They were moments of radical honesty from a body that could no longer maintain the lie. They were my nervous system saying, "Enough. We cannot do this anymore."

And in those moments of crisis, something remarkable happened. The world didn't end when I couldn't be strong. People didn't leave when I couldn't be funny. The ground didn't open up and swallow me when I admitted I wasn't okay.

In fact, the opposite occurred. An authentic connection became possible. Real support emerged. Genuine intimacy developed, not despite but because of my vulnerability.

Dr Brené Brown's research confirms this: vulnerability isn't weakness. It's the most accurate measure of courage, and it's the birthplace of connection, creativity, and wholeness.

My body knew this before my mind did. It forced the issue when my ego wasn't ready to surrender the mask. It created symptoms I couldn't ignore, feelings I couldn't suppress, reactions I couldn't control, all in service of bringing me back to authenticity.

Reflection: The Journey Back to Authenticity

The journey from mask to authenticity isn't a single dramatic moment. There are thousands of small choices: to be real instead of impressive, present instead of perfect, and honest instead of comfortable.

It's learning to sit with discomfort rather than joke it away. It's allowing silence instead of filling it with noise. It's saying, "I don't know," "I'm struggling," or "I need help", when every instinct screams to maintain the illusion of having it all together.

And it's physical work as much as emotional work. It's noticing the tension in your jaw and consciously relaxing it. It's feeling the knot in your stomach and breathing into it rather than ignoring it. It's recognising the shallow breathing of anxiety and deliberately taking deeper breaths.

It's reclaiming your body as a source of wisdom rather than an inconvenient container for your performing self.

This doesn't mean never using humour, never being strong, never putting on a brave face when the situation calls for it. It means doing these things consciously, by choice, rather than as an automatic trauma response. It means accessing your full range of emotional expression rather than being stuck in one adaptive pattern.

The body doesn't lie, and when we learn to listen to it, we discover a truth more powerful than any mask: we are already enough, exactly as we are.

Reflection Prompt: What mask do you wear most often? How does it feel in your body when you're wearing this mask? Can you identify physical sensations that might be

Zelda Marsh

telling you when the mask is becoming too heavy to carry?

Chapter 8: The Nervous System's Language

Zelda Marsh

The Body's Secret Code

If you've ever wondered why you can't just "think" your way out of trauma, here's your answer: trauma doesn't live in the thinking part of your brain. It lives in your nervous system, that complex network of nerves that runs through your entire body like the world's most complicated electrical wiring. And let me tell you, when that wiring gets crossed, no amount of positive affirmations or logical reasoning will sort it out.

I spent years trying to convince myself I was "fine" after everything that happened. I'd repeat mantras in the mirror, read self-help books, and try to rationalise away my reactions. "It was years ago," I'd tell myself. "Just get over it already." But my body had other ideas. My racing heart, churning stomach, and constant state of hypervigilance weren't interested in my rational arguments.

That's because trauma speaks a different language: the language of the nervous system. And if you want to heal, you must become fluent in that language.

Dr. Stephen Porges, the neurologist who developed the Polyvagal Theory, explains that our nervous system has three main states: ventral vagal (safe and social), sympathetic (fight or flight), and dorsal vagal (freeze or collapse). These states aren't chosen consciously; they're automatic responses designed to keep us alive in the face of threat.

For those of us with trauma, our nervous system gets stuck in sympathetic or dorsal vagal states, constantly perceiving threats even in safe environments. It's like having a faulty smoke alarm that goes off when someone makes toast. Bloody, annoying, and impossible to ignore.

Understanding this was a game-changer for me. It wasn't that I was weak, broken, or "too sensitive." My nervous system was doing exactly what it was designed to do: protect me. The problem was that it was working with outdated information, still responding to no longer present dangers.

Fight, Flight, Freeze, and Fawn: The Four F's of Trauma Response

When I first learned about the four F's of trauma response, it was like someone had been secretly observing me my entire life and taking detailed notes. Suddenly, so many of my seemingly random behaviours made perfect sense.

Fight: This is the "I'll come at you before you come at me" response. For me, this showed up as being quick to anger, defensive, and argumentative. I'd pick fights with partners over nothing, always ready to pounce on the slightest perceived criticism. It wasn't that I was just a moody cow; my nervous system was trying to protect me by attacking first.

Flight: The "get me the hell out of here" response. This manifested as my tendency to bail on relationships the moment they got difficult, change jobs frequently, and move houses, cities, and even countries when things got uncomfortable. It also showed up in smaller ways, leaving parties early, avoiding specific conversations, and keeping myself constantly busy so I didn't have to feel anything.

Freeze: The "play dead, and maybe the predator will lose interest" response. This was me dissociating during arguments, going blank during stressful situations, and feeling like I was watching myself from outside my body. It was the numbness that would descend when emotions got too intense, the way I'd sometimes find myself staring into space, lost in a fog of disconnection.

Fawn: The "I'll be whatever you want me to be, just please don't hurt me" response. This was perhaps my most well-developed trauma response—people-pleasing, shape-shifting, abandoning my own needs to keep others happy. I became whoever I thought others wanted me to be, a chameleon changing colours to blend into any environment, desperate for approval and terrified of rejection.

These responses weren't character flaws or personal failings. They were survival mechanisms developed in response to trauma. They had kept me safe when I was in danger, but now they were preventing me from living a whole life.

Dr. Pete Walker, in his book "Complex PTSD: From Surviving to Thriving," explains that these four responses are adaptive when we're in actual danger but become problematic when they're activated in situations where there is no real threat. They become habitual ways of responding to the world, keeping us trapped in patterns that no longer serve us.

The tricky part is that these responses happen automatically, below the level of conscious awareness. I wasn't choosing to people-please, dissociate, or run away from intimacy. My nervous system made those choices for me based on its primary directive: keep this human alive at all costs.

The Vagus Nerve: Your Body's Information Superhighway

If the nervous system has a CEO, it's the vagus nerve. This cranial nerve runs from your brainstem down through your body, influencing everything from your heart rate and digestion to your ability to connect with others. It's like the information superhighway of your body, carrying messages back and forth between your brain and your organs.

The vagus nerve plays a crucial role in regulating the stress response. When it's functioning well, it helps you return to a state of calm after danger has passed. But as we have learned, trauma can disrupt this process, leaving your vagus nerve stuck in a state of high alert.

Dr Deb Dana, author of "The Polyvagal Theory in Therapy," describes the vagus nerve as having two branches: the ventral vagal branch, which helps us feel safe and connected, and the dorsal vagal branch, which activates our freeze response when we're in extreme danger.

For those of us with trauma, our vagal tone, the health and responsiveness of our vagus nerve, is often compromised. We might have difficulty accessing the ventral vagal state of safety and connection, instead bouncing between sympathetic arousal (fight/flight) and dorsal vagal collapse (freeze).

I noticed this in my own body. When I felt threatened (which was often, given my hypervigilant nervous system), I'd either go into fight mode, heart racing, muscles tense, ready to defend myself or collapse into a state of numbness and disconnection, unable to think clearly or advocate for myself.

Learning about the vagus nerve helped me understand why certain practices were helpful for my healing. Deep breathing, humming, singing, and cold water on my face weren't just random self-care activities; they directly stimulate my vagus nerve, helping regulate my nervous system and bring me back to a state of safety.

It also explained why talk therapy alone had limited effectiveness for me. I could understand my trauma intellectually, but if my nervous system was still dysregulated, that understanding didn't translate into lasting change. I needed approaches that spoke directly to my nervous system and helped retrain my vagus nerve to recognise safety.

Hypervigilance: Always on Guard

One of the most exhausting aspects of living with trauma is the constant state of hypervigilance. It's like being a security guard who never gets to clock out, constantly scanning for threats, always on high alert.

For me, hypervigilance looked like:

- Walking into a room and immediately identifying all exits
- Sitting with my back to the wall in restaurants
- Startling at sudden noises
- Constantly monitoring other people's facial expressions and tone of voice for signs of anger or disapproval.
- Difficulty sleeping because my brain wouldn't switch off
- Physical tension, especially in my shoulders and jaw
- Interpreting neutral comments as criticism or attacks

It was exhausting, this constant state of readiness. And the worst part was, I didn't even realise I was doing it. This perpetual state of alertness was so normal to me that I didn't know there was any other way to be.

In "The Body Keeps the Score," Dr. Bessel van der Kolk explains hypervigilance as a common trauma symptom. The amygdala, the brain's alarm system, becomes overactive, constantly scanning for danger and triggering stress responses even in safe situations.

This hypervigilance affected every aspect of my life. It made it difficult to relax, trust others, and be present in the moment. It kept me in a state of chronic stress, which took a toll on my physical health, contributing to digestive issues, tension headaches, and chronic fatigue.

It also made it nearly impossible to form healthy relationships. It's hard to let people in when you're constantly on guard, expecting danger around every corner. I'd analyse every text message for hidden meanings, interpret silence as rejection, and assume the worst intentions behind innocent actions. It's no wonder my relationships were characterised by anxiety and conflict.

The irony is that hypervigilance is meant to keep us safe, but it prevents us from recognising when we are safe. It's like wearing sunglasses indoors and then complaining that it's too dark to see properly. My nervous system was so focused on spotting danger that it filtered out all evidence of safety and connection.

Triggers: When the Past Invades the Present

Triggers are perhaps the most obvious way our nervous system speaks to us about unresolved trauma. A trigger in the present reminds our nervous system of past danger, causing it to activate a stress response as if that danger were happening right now.

Triggers can be obvious, a backfiring car that sounds like a gunshot, a raised voice that reminds us of an abusive parent. But they can also be subtle, a certain smell, a particular phrase, even a time of year.

My triggers were numerous and often confusing. The smell of a certain aftershave would send my heart racing. Being touched unexpectedly, even gently, could cause me to freeze or lash out. Specific phrases, "Don't be so sensitive" or "You're overreacting", would trigger a flood of shame and anger that seemed disproportionate to the situation.

For years, I thought I was "too emotional" or "couldn't take a joke." I didn't realise these were trauma responses, my nervous system reacting to perceived threats based on past experiences.

Dr. Janina Fisher, in her book "Healing the Fragmented Selves of Trauma Survivors," explains that triggers activate implicit memory, the body's memory of trauma, which is different from explicit, narrative memory. When we're triggered, we're not remembering the trauma in a conscious, storytelling way; we're reliving it in our bodies, experiencing the same physiological responses we had during the original traumatic event.

This explained why my reactions to triggers felt so overwhelming and out of my control. It wasn't just that I was thinking about past trauma; my body was actually re-experiencing it, flooding with the same stress hormones, activating the same defensive responses.

Understanding triggers as nervous system responses rather than personal weaknesses was liberating. It meant I wasn't "crazy" or "too sensitive." My body was doing exactly what bodies do when they've experienced trauma, trying to keep me safe by responding to perceived threats.

It also gave me a roadmap for healing. If triggers were my nervous system's way of speaking to me about unresolved trauma, then learning to work with triggers—to stay present with them, to soothe my nervous system when they occur could be a path toward integration and healing.

Dissociation: The Ultimate Escape Hatch

When fight, flight, and even freeze aren't options, the nervous system has one more trick: dissociation. This is the mind's ability to disconnect from the present moment, to separate consciousness from the body, and to create distance from overwhelming experiences.

Dissociation exists on a spectrum. At the mild end, there's daydreaming or "zoning out." At the extreme end, there are dissociative disorders where people experience significant detachment from their identity, memories, or surroundings.

For trauma survivors, dissociation is often a well-developed survival mechanism. Psychological escape becomes the next best option when physical escape isn't possible.

My own experiences with dissociation were varied. Sometimes, it was subtle. I found myself driving on autopilot, arriving at my destination with no memory of the journey. Other times, it was more pronounced. I felt like I was floating above my body during arguments, watching myself from a distance as if I were a character in a film.

During particularly stressful situations, I'd experience what therapists call "emotional numbing", a complete absence of feeling, as if someone had turned down the volume on my emotions until they were barely audible.

Dr. Pat Ogden, founder of Sensorimotor Psychotherapy, describes dissociation as "the nervous system's emergency brake." When the accelerator of hyperarousal (fight/flight) is pressed at the same time as the brake of hyperarousal (freeze), the system can't handle the contradiction, and dissociation occurs.

For me, dissociation has been a lifesaver during traumatic experiences. It allowed me to endure what would otherwise have been unbearable. But like other trauma responses, it had outlived its usefulness. It was now preventing me from being fully present in my life, feeling the full range of human emotions, and connecting deeply with others.

Healing dissociation involved learning to recognise when I was disconnecting and developing tools to gently bring myself back to the present moment. Grounding techniques like feeling my feet on the floor, naming objects I could see, or holding something cold helped anchor me in my body when I floated away.

It also involved gradually increasing my "window of tolerance", the range of arousal within which I could function effectively without resorting to fight, flight, freeze, or dissociation. This meant slowly exposing myself to triggering situations while using regulation tools to stay present, gradually teaching my nervous system that it could handle discomfort without shutting down.

Zelda Marsh

THIS IS THE BEAT: Somatic Symptoms: The Body's Distress Signals

It remains to be one of the most challenging aspects of trauma, the way it manifests in physical symptoms that seem unrelated to psychological distress. These somatic symptoms, physical manifestations of emotional pain, are the body's way of communicating what the mind cannot or will not acknowledge.

My own body had been sending me distress signals for years, but I'd been too busy trying to "think positive" to listen. I had:

- Chronic digestive issues that no diet seemed to fix
- Tension headaches and jaw pain from constantly clenching
- Unexplained rashes and skin irritations
- Frequent colds and infections from a compromised immune system
- Chronic fatigue that no amount of sleep could remedy
- Muscle pain and stiffness, especially in my shoulders and neck

I'd been to countless doctors and tried numerous medications and treatments, but nothing provided lasting relief. That's because I was treating the symptoms without addressing the root cause: my dysregulated nervous system.

Dr. Gabor Maté, in his book "When the Body Says No," explains that chronic stress and trauma can manifest as physical illness. The constant flood of stress hormones takes a toll on the body, compromising immune function, disrupting digestion, and creating inflammation.

For me, understanding the connection between my physical symptoms and my trauma was both validating and empowering. It meant I wasn't imagining things or being a hypochondriac. My body was genuinely in distress, trying desperately to get my attention.

It also meant that healing my trauma could potentially alleviate my physical symptoms. Indeed, as I began to work with my nervous system, to process my trauma, and to learn regulation skills, many of my somatic symptoms started to improve. Not overnight, and not completely, but enough to confirm that I was on the right track.

This mind-body connection is now well-established in scientific research. Studies have shown links between trauma and conditions like irritable bowel syndrome, fibromyalgia, chronic fatigue syndrome, and autoimmune disorders. The ACE (Adverse Childhood Experiences) study, one of the most extensive investigations into childhood abuse and neglect, found a strong correlation between early trauma and later health problems.

As Dr. van der Kolk says, the body keeps the score. And sometimes, it tallies that score in the form of physical symptoms that conventional medicine struggles to explain or treat effectively.

Zelda Marsh

Nervous System Regulation: The Key to Healing

If trauma dysregulates the nervous system, then healing involves learning to regulate it again to expand our window of tolerance, to recognise when we're in fight/flight or freeze, and to develop tools for returning to a state of safety and connection.

This is where the concept of "bottom-up" healing comes in. Traditional talk therapy often takes a "top-down" approach, starting with cognitive understanding and hoping it will trickle down to change emotional and physiological responses. However, for trauma, A bottom-up approach, starting with the body and nervous system and then working up to cognitive understanding, is often more effective.

Dr. Peter Levine, developer of Somatic Experiencing, emphasises the importance of this bottom-up approach. He explains that trauma is primarily a physiological experience, stored in the body, and therefore healing must involve the body.

For me, nervous system regulation began with simply learning to recognise my different states. What did it feel like in my body when I was in fight/flight mode? What about freeze? What sensations signalled that I was moving toward dissociation? This awareness was the first step toward choice. I couldn't change what I couldn't recognise.

Then came the practice of regulating skills, tools, and techniques for bringing my nervous system back into balance when it became dysregulated. These included:

- Deep, diaphragmatic breathing to activate the parasympathetic nervous system
- Progressive muscle relaxation to release physical tension
- Grounding techniques to bring me back to the present moment
- Movement to discharge the energy of the fight/flight
- Self-compassion practices to counter the shame that often accompanies dysregulation
- Connection with safe others to co-regulate (more on this later)

I practised these skills daily, not just when I was in distress. Like any skill, nervous system regulation requires consistent practice to become second nature. I was retraining my nervous system, teaching it that it was safe to relax, that not every stimulus was a threat, and that it could return to balance after activation.

This wasn't quick or easy work. My nervous system had spent decades in a state of dysregulation; it wouldn't change overnight. There were setbacks when I felt like I was making no progress. But gradually, almost imperceptibly, things began to shift.

I could stay present during difficult conversations instead of dissociating. I could feel triggered without being completely overwhelmed by the sensation. I could recognise when I was moving into fight/flight and take steps to regulate before I said or did something I'd regret.

These might seem like small victories, but they were revolutionary for someone whose nervous system had been in chaos for most of their life.

Co-Regulation: We Heal in Connection

One of the most powerful discoveries in my healing journey was the concept of co-regulation—the idea that our nervous systems are designed to regulate in connection with others. Just as trauma often occurs in relationships, healing usually happens in relationships, too.

Dr. Stephen Porges explains that our nervous systems constantly communicate with each other through what he calls "neuroception"—the unconscious assessment of safety or danger in our environment, including the people around us. When we're with someone whose nervous system is regulated, our own nervous system tends to synchronise with theirs, moving toward regulation as well.

This explained why I felt so calm in the presence of certain people and so anxious around others. It wasn't just about their words or actions; it was about the state of their nervous system and how it was influencing mine.

It also explained why isolation had always made my symptoms worse. Without the co-regulating presence of others, my nervous system had no external reference point for safety, no model for regulation.

Learning to co-regulate involved several components:

- Identifying people who had a regulating effect on my nervous system
- Spending time with these people, especially when I was feeling dysregulated
- Being vulnerable about my struggles rather than hiding them
- Allowing others to support me rather than insisting on self-sufficiency
- Practising regulation skills together, such as synchronised breathing or movement

This wasn't about becoming dependent on others for my well-being. It was about recognising that humans are social creatures designed to regulate the community. Just as a child learns to regulate their emotions through interactions with caregivers, adults continue to regulate through connection with others.

The beauty of co-regulation is that it's mutual. As I learned to regulate my nervous system, I became better able to offer co-regulation to others. This created a positive feedback loop, where my relationships became sources of healing rather than additional stress.

The Language of Sensation: Learning to Listen to Your Body

One of the most challenging aspects of working with the nervous system is learning to tune into bodily sensations: the language the nervous system communicates with. For many trauma survivors, disconnection from the body is a well-established coping mechanism. Feeling sensations might have been too overwhelming or painful, so we learned to numb and live from the neck up.

This was certainly true for me. I was excellent at analysing, rationalising, and intellectualising, but I'd draw a blank when asked what I felt in my body. It was as if a thick fog between my consciousness and physical sensations made accessing or interpreting my body's signals difficult.

Dr Pat Ogden describes this as "sensory amnesia", the inability to feel or identify bodily sensations due to trauma. This disconnection serves a protective function during traumatic experiences, but becomes problematic when it persists afterwards, preventing us from accessing the very information we need to heal.

Learning to reconnect with my body was a slow, sometimes uncomfortable process. It began with simply noticing sensations without judgment or interpretation. What did I feel in my chest, stomach, throat, and hands? Was there tension, tingling, warmth, coolness, pressure, or emptiness?

At first, this practice would often trigger anxiety or dissociation, my nervous system's habitual response to bodily awareness. But with patience and persistence, I gradually developed the capacity to stay present with sensations, to be curious about them rather than afraid of them.

As I became more fluent in the language of sensation, I discovered that my body had been trying to communicate with me all along. The tightness in my chest wasn't just random discomfort; it was anxiety signalling a perceived threat. The heaviness in my limbs wasn't just fatigue; it was my body moving into a freeze response. The churning in my stomach wasn't just digestive issues; it was my nervous system responding to social stress.

This awareness gave me valuable information about my internal state, allowing me to respond skilfully, rather than react automatically. If I noticed my heart racing and my muscles tensing, I could recognise that I was moving into fight/flight and take steps to regulate before I became completely dysregulated.

It also allowed me to track my progress in healing. As my nervous system began to regulate, I noticed changes in my physical sensations, less chronic tension, more ease in my body, and a greater capacity to feel pleasure and relaxation.

The Healing Journey: From Dysregulation to Resilience

Healing from trauma isn't about never getting dysregulated again. It's about developing the capacity to return to regulation more quickly and effectively when dysregulation occurs. It's about expanding our window of tolerance so that we can experience a broader range of emotions without becoming overwhelmed. It's about building resilience, the ability to bounce back from adversity.

Dr. Dan Siegel, a clinical professor of psychiatry, defines resilience as "the capacity to face challenges and become more, not less, engaged with life." This doesn't mean struggling or suffering; it means having the resources to move through difficulty without becoming stuck in it.

For me, resilience has looked like:

- Being able to feel triggered without being completely overwhelmed by the sensation
- Recognising when I'm moving into fight/flight/freeze/fawn and taking steps to regulate
- Staying present during difficult conversations instead of dissociating
- Recovering more quickly from setbacks and disappointments
- Being able to feel vulnerable emotions like sadness and fear without being consumed by them
- Having a wider range of responses to stress, rather than defaulting to my habitual trauma responses

This resilience didn't develop overnight. It resulted from consistent practice, learning to work with my nervous system rather than against it, and building a toolbox of regulation skills I could use when dysregulation occurred.

It also involved developing what Dr Richard Schwartz, founder of Internal Family Systems Therapy, calls "self-leadership", the capacity to maintain a compassionate, curious relationship with all parts of myself, including the parts that carry trauma. Rather than fighting against my trauma responses or being ashamed of them, I learned to understand them as protective mechanisms that had helped me survive.

This self-leadership allowed me to respond to dysregulation with compassion rather than criticism. Instead of berating myself for being "too sensitive" or "overreacting," I could acknowledge that my nervous system was doing what it had learned to do to keep me safe. I could thank these protective parts for their efforts while gently guiding them toward more effective strategies in the present.

The Ongoing Conversation

Working with the nervous system isn't a one-time fix; it's an ongoing conversation. Just as we continue to have new experiences that shape our nervous system throughout life, we continue to have opportunities to choose how we respond to those experiences.

There are still days when my nervous system gets hijacked by a trigger when I find myself in fight/flight or freeze, despite all my regulation skills. The difference now is that I don't see these moments as failures or setbacks. They're simply opportunities to practice, strengthen the neural pathways of regulation, and deepen my relationship with my nervous system.

I've also come to appreciate the wisdom of my nervous system, even in its dysregulated state. My fight response protects my boundaries. My flight response removes me from harmful situations. My freeze response conserves energy when action isn't possible. My fawn response helps me navigate social complexities. These responses aren't inherently bad; they're sometimes applied in situations that are not helpful.

The goal isn't to eliminate these responses but to guide them by my prefrontal cortex, the part of my brain responsible for executive function, decision-making, and social behaviour. This allows me to choose my responses rather than being driven by automatic reactions.

Dr Bonnie Badenoch, author of "The Heart of Trauma," describes this as developing a "wise, compassionate witness" to our experience, a part of us that can observe our nervous system states without being completely identified. This witness allows us to say, "I notice I'm feeling triggered right now," rather than being triggered.

This capacity for self-observation creates space between stimulus and response, between trigger and reaction. And in that space lies freedom, the freedom to choose how we respond rather than being at the mercy of our automatic nervous system reactions.

Learning the Language, Speaking It Fluently

Learning the language of the nervous system has been one of the most challenging and rewarding aspects of my healing journey. It's required patience, persistence, and a willingness to feel sensations that I'd spent years avoiding. It meant developing a new relationship with my body based on listening and respect rather than control and disconnection.

But the rewards have been immeasurable. As I've become more fluent in this language, I've gained access to a wealth of information about my internal state, needs, boundaries, and capacity for connection. I've developed a more nuanced understanding of my reactions and a greater ability to respond skillfully to life's challenges.

I've also discovered that this language isn't just about trauma and healing; it's about the full spectrum of human experience. The same nervous system that can become dysregulated in response to threat can also experience profound joy, connection, and peace. As I've learned to regulate my nervous system, I've also gained access to these positive states.

This is the most beautiful aspect of working with the nervous system: it's not just about reducing suffering but expanding our capacity for aliveness. It's about being able to feel the full range of human emotions, to be present with our experience, whatever it may be, to engage fully with the messy, magnificent business of being human.

So, if you're on this journey of learning your nervous system's language, be patient with yourself. It's a complex language, with dialects and nuances that take time to master. But it's also your native tongue, the first language you ever spoke, before words, concepts, and stories. Your body remembers it, even if your conscious mind has forgotten.

And when you begin to speak it fluently again, you'll discover that your nervous system has been trying to tell you something all along: that beneath the layers of protection and adaptation, beyond the trauma responses and coping mechanisms, there is a fundamental capacity for regulation, resilience, and connection that has been there all along, waiting to be remembered.

Zelda Marsh

PART THREE: RECLAMATION & HEALING

Finding freedom without forgiveness

Chapter 9: The Breaking Point

Zelda Marsh

The Kitchen Floor Epiphany

There's a moment in every healing journey that changes everything. It's the moment when you can't keep pretending anymore, when the masks crack, and when the body says, "Enough."

For some, it's dramatic, a complete breakdown, a hospital stay, a crisis that can't be ignored. For others, it's quieter a morning when you can't get out of bed, a panic attack in the supermarket, a moment when you look in the mirror and don't recognise the person staring back.

Mine? It happened in my kitchen on an ordinary Tuesday while making a bloody cup of tea.

I'd been running on empty for years, working myself to the bone, being everything to everyone, the perfect mum, supportive friend, reliable colleague, strong one who never needed help.

I was exhausted. Not just tired soul-level, bone-deep, can't-remember-what-rest-feels-like exhausted. But I kept going. Because that's what I'd always done, keep going. Push through. Survive.

That Tuesday morning, I put the kettle on like I always did. Reached for a mug. And then… nothing. My hand froze mid-air. My chest tightened. The room started spinning. And before I knew what was happening, I was on the kitchen floor, sobbing like the world was ending.

And in a way, it was. The world I'd constructed, the one where I was fine, where I could handle anything, where trauma was something I'd "dealt with" years ago, that world was crumbling around me.

I sat there for hours. Couldn't move. Couldn't call anyone. Just sat with my back against the cupboards, knees pulled to my chest, crying until there was nothing left.

It wasn't sadness, exactly. It was grief. Rage. Relief. Terror. Every emotion I'd ever swallowed down, rising like a tsunami, I couldn't outrun anymore.

My body had finally said, "No more."

And for once in my life, I listened.

The Body's Ultimatum

What I didn't understand then but research makes clear now is that my body had been sending warning signals for years. The migraines. The digestive issues. Chronic fatigue. The mysterious rashes. Insomnia.

These weren't random health problems. They were distress signals from a nervous system in crisis.

Dr Gabor Maté explains this phenomenon in his book "When the Body Says No." He describes how the body eventually forces us to address what the mind refuses to acknowledge. It's like a child trying to get a parent's attention—first, it whispers, then it speaks, then it shouts, and finally, when all else fails, it throws a full-blown tantrum.

My body had been whispering for decades. That morning in the kitchen, it was done whispering. It was screaming.

According to Dr. Peter Levine, creator of Somatic Experiencing therapy, this kind of breakdown is often a breakthrough. The nervous system finally releases energy trapped for years, sometimes decades. It's not a sign of weakness or failure. It's the beginning of genuine healing.

But God, it didn't feel like healing at the time. It felt like dying.

The False Starts

After my kitchen floor moment, I did what many of us do: I looked for quick fixes.

Anything to make the pain stop.

Anything to feel normal again.

I tried meditation apps that promised peace in ten minutes a day. I bought self-help books with titles like "Heal Your Life in 30 Days!" I signed up for wellness retreats where beautiful people in linen clothes talked about manifesting abundance while I sat in the back, wondering if they'd ever actually experienced trauma.

I tried positive affirmations in the mirror: " Choose happiness, " " Just let it go."

And when none of that worked? I tried numbing. Wine o'clock started earlier and earlier. Netflix binges lasted longer. I shopped for things I didn't need. Ate foods that made me feel worse. Scrolled social media until my eyes burned.

I was doing everything except the one thing I needed to do: face the truth.

The truth is that I wasn't OK. That I'd never been OK. Those decades of trauma were living in my body, and no amount of positive thinking was going to erase them magically.

The truth was that healing wasn't going to be pretty or Instagram-worthy. It was going to be messy, painful, and raw.

The truth is that I couldn't do it alone.

The Moment of Surrender

Real healing began the day I stopped trying to heal.

Sounds contradictory. But it's true. As long as I was chasing healing, trying to force it, schedule it, and control it, I was still operating from the same trauma responses that had governed my entire life.

Healing began when I surrendered, admitted I didn't have the answers, and acknowledged that the strategies that had kept me alive for decades were now keeping me from truly living.

It was terrifying. Because who was I, if not the strong one? Who was I, if not the survivor? Who would I be if I actually let myself be vulnerable, messy, and human?

I didn't know. And that was the point.

Dr Brené Brown talks about this as "the reckoning," the moment when we stop running from our pain and turn to face it. It's not a single decision but a practice of courage, choosing truth over comfort again and again.

For me, surrender looked like this: sitting in a therapist's office, hands shaking, voice barely above a whisper, saying the words I'd never allowed myself to say out loud.

"I'm not OK. I've never been OK. And I don't know how to be OK."

It was the most honest thing I'd ever said. And it was the beginning of everything.

The Body Awakening

The following physical awakening was one of the most profound aspects of my breaking point. After decades of disconnection from my body, of treating it as something to ignore, override, or control, I began to feel again.

And holy hell, was it uncomfortable.

I started noticing sensations I'd been blocking out for years: the constant tension in my jaw, the shallow breathing, the way my shoulders lived somewhere around my ears, and the knot in my stomach that never fully relaxed.

I became aware of how I held my breath during difficult conversations, how certain people's voices made my heart race, and how specific memories could trigger a full-body freeze response.

This heightened awareness wasn't pleasant; it was excruciating at times, but it was also the first step toward genuine healing.

Dr. Bessel van der Kolk explains that trauma survivors often dissociate from their bodies as a protective mechanism. It's too painful to inhabit a body that holds so much unprocessed trauma fully. However, this disconnection, while protective in the short term, prevents healing in the long term.

Reconnecting with the body, learning to feel again, listening to its signals, and being present with its sensations is essential for trauma recovery. Not because it's comfortable, but because it's real.

And after a lifetime of pretending reality, however painful, it felt like a revelation.

The Grief Tsunami

Once I started feeling again, the grief came in waves. Not just sadness for what had happened to me, but mourning for all the years I'd lost. I wasted all the energy trying to be OK when I wasn't. All the relationships had suffered because I couldn't be authentic.

I grieved for the little girl with the twisted legs who never got the support she needed. For the five/six-year-old whose violation was met with silence. For the teenager who carried burdens that no child should bear. For the young woman who thought abuse was what she deserved.

I grieved for all the times I'd abandoned myself because I'd been taught that my needs didn't matter. All the times, I'd silenced my own voice because I'd learned it wouldn't be heard anyway.

This grief wasn't neat or linear. It didn't follow the five stages they taught you in psychology class. It was chaotic, unpredictable, and all-consuming. Some days, I could function. On other days, I could barely get out of bed.

And that was OK. Because for the first time, I wasn't trying to rush through the pain or package it into something palatable. I allowed it to be exactly what it was: messy, raw, honest.

Dr. Jonice Webb, who specialises in childhood emotional neglect, explains that this kind of delayed grief is common among those who weren't allowed to process emotions as children. When we're finally safe enough to feel, years or even decades of suppressed grief can emerge all at once.

It's not a sign that something's wrong. It's a sign that healing has begun.

The Rage Revelation

And then came the rage. Not polite anger. Not mild irritation. Pure, unadulterated, primal rage.

Rage at the twelve-year-old boy who violated me. At my mother, who betrayed my trust. At the adults who saw but didn't intervene. At the systems that failed to protect me. At the culture that taught me to stay silent.

Rage at myself for all the ways I'd abandoned my own needs. For the relationships I'd accepted that were far less than I deserved. For the boundaries, I'd failed to set. For the times I'd said yes when every cell in my body was screaming no.

This anger terrified me at first. I'd spent my entire life being "nice," swallowing rage, smoothing things over. Anger made me like my mother: volatile, unpredictable, dangerous, or so I believed.

But this rage was different. It wasn't destructive. It was clarifying. It wasn't about hurting others. It was about finally acknowledging how much I'd been hurt.

In her book The Dance of Anger, Dr. Harriet Lerner describes anger as a signal that something is wrong, that a boundary has been crossed, and that change is needed. For women, especially, anger is often pathologised and dismissed as "being emotional" or "overreacting."

But my anger wasn't an overreaction. If anything, it was decades overdue.

One of the most transformative aspects of my healing journey was learning to feel this anger, express it safely, listen to its wisdom, and let it fuel positive change rather than destruction.

Because anger, when channelled constructively, isn't the opposite of healing. It's often the catalyst for it.

The Identity Crisis

As I moved through grief and rage, I hit another challenge: the identity crisis. Who was I, if not the survivor? The strong one? The one who had it all together?

My entire identity had been built around trauma responses. Hypervigilance had made me observant. People-pleasing had made me empathetic. Dissociation had made me creative. These weren't just coping mechanisms but the foundation of how I saw myself.

As I began to heal, as these responses became less necessary for survival, I felt like I was losing parts of myself. Would I still be intuitive if I weren't hypervigilant? Would I still care about others if I weren't a people pleaser? Would I still be creative if I weren't escaping reality?

This identity crisis is what psychologists call "post-traumatic growth pains." As we heal from trauma, we have to reimagine who we are beyond our wounds. We have to discover who we might have been if the trauma hadn't shaped us, while also honouring how it did.

It's like renovating a house, messy and disruptive while you live in it. Sometimes, it feels like everything is falling apart. But it's the only way to build something new without abandoning what came before.

For me, this meant recognising that my strengths weren't created by trauma; they existed despite it. My empathy wasn't a trauma response; it was who I was at my core, though trauma had twisted it into people-pleasing. My creativity wasn't just escapism; it was my soul's expression, though trauma had sometimes hijacked it for survival.

Healing didn't mean losing these qualities. It meant reclaiming them, using them by choice rather than compulsion, and expressing them from a place of wholeness rather than woundedness.

The Support Revolution

The most radical act in my breaking point journey was asking for help, not offering it. I'd been doing that my whole life, but actually asking for it, needing it, and receiving it.

This went against everything I'd been taught and believed about myself. Strong people don't need help.

Survivors handle things on their own. Asking for support is a weakness.

But here's what I learned: those beliefs weren't true. They were trauma-talking.

The truth is that humans are wired for connection. We're not meant to heal in isolation. The nervous system regulates through relationships, which neuroscientists call "co-regulation." We need other people not because we're weak but because we're human.

Finding the proper support wasn't easy. Not everyone can hold space for trauma. Not everyone understands the complexity of healing. I had to be discerning. I had to learn the difference between those who could truly support me and those who just wanted to fix, save, or use my vulnerability to feel better about themselves.

I found a trauma-informed therapist who understood the body's role in healing, joined support groups where I didn't have to explain or justify my experiences, and connected with friends who could sit with discomfort without trying to sugarcoat it away.

Perhaps most importantly, I learned to be my own support, treat myself with the same compassion I'd always offered others, speak to myself with kindness rather than criticism, and trust my experience rather than constantly seeking external validation.

This revolution in support changed everything. It showed me that needing others doesn't make me weak; it makes me human. That vulnerability isn't a liability; it's the pathway to genuine connection. I don't have to earn love by being useful; I'm worthy of it simply because I exist.

Zelda Marsh

The Body as Ally, Not Enemy

My relationship with my body transformed as my breaking point evolved into a breakthrough. After decades of seeing it as unreliable, problematic, something to be controlled or ignored, I began to recognise it as my greatest ally in healing.

My body had never lied to me. It had been trying to communicate through symptoms, sensations, and intuitive hits. The problem wasn't my body's messages; I'd been taught to dismiss them.

I started simple practices to rebuild this relationship: breathing consciously, moving intuitively rather than pushing through prescribed exercises, and asking my body what it needed instead of telling it what it should do.

I learned to track sensations to notice what happened in my body during different situations and with different people. I discovered that my body would signal "no" long before my mind could articulate a tightening in my throat, a heaviness in my chest, a sinking in my stomach.

Similarly, it would signal "yes" with warmth, expansion, and ease of breath. These weren't just random physical responses but wisdom, intelligence, and guidance.

Dr. Peter Levine calls this "felt sense", the body's way of communicating information that the conscious mind might miss or dismiss. Learning to access this felt sense, trust it, and let it guide decisions is a cornerstone of trauma healing.

It meant finally having an internal compass after decades of looking outside myself for direction. It meant recognising that my body wasn't broken, it was brilliantly adaptive. It had kept me alive through circumstances that could have destroyed me.

The very symptoms I'd resented, the anxiety, the hypervigilance, the digestive issues, the chronic pain, were evidence not of weakness but of extraordinary resilience. They were my body doing everything it could to protect me when no one else would.

The Spiritual Awakening

My breaking point wasn't just psychological; it was spiritual. Not in a religious sense, though that's valid, too. But in the sense of reconnecting with something larger than myself, something that had been there all along, waiting for me to notice.

Remember those childhood moments I mentioned earlier? The blackbirds that seemed to watch over me. The fox that sat with me while I cried. The butterflies in winter. The feeling of a hand on my back when no one was there.

As I healed, these experiences didn't diminish; they deepened. I began to recognise them not as coincidences or imagination but as evidence of a connection of being held by something beyond what I could see or touch.

This wasn't about escaping reality through spiritual bypassing. It wasn't about using spirituality to avoid doing the hard work of healing. It was about expanding my understanding of reality to include dimensions I'd been taught to dismiss.

The synchronicities increased, the dreams became more vivid, and the sense of guidance became more tangible, not because I was special, but because I was finally listening.

This spiritual dimension gave context to my suffering, not in an "everything happens for a reason" way, I reject that kind of toxic positivity, but in recognising that my pain, while real and valid, wasn't the totality of who I was. There was an essence that had never been damaged beneath the trauma and beyond the wounds.

Call it soul, spirit, authentic self, higher consciousness, the name doesn't matter. What matters is the experience of reconnecting with a part of myself that trauma couldn't touch. That existed before the wounds and would exist after the healing.

This wasn't about transcending my humanity but embracing it fully, including the messy, painful parts, the broken places where, as Leonard Cohen wrote, "the light gets in."

Reflection: Your Own Breaking Point

Breaking points aren't failures: they're invitations. They are opportunities to finally stop running from what's true, face what needs facing, and begin the journey home to yourself.

Your breaking point might not look like mine. It might be louder or quieter. More dramatic or more subtle. It might come as a crisis or a whisper. But if you're reading this, chances are you've either experienced it already or are on the edge of it now.

Either way, I want you to know you're not falling apart. You're breaking open. And on the other side of this shattering is a wholeness you can't yet imagine.

The question isn't whether you'll have a breaking point. The question is what you'll do when it comes. Will you run from it? Numb it? Deny it? Or will you turn toward it with all the courage it requires and allow it to transform you?

That's the paradox of healing: sometimes, we must break before becoming whole.

Reflection Prompt: Have you experienced a breaking point in your healing journey?

Where in your body did you feel it most intensely?

If you haven't yet reached this point, where do you resist letting go of control of your body?

Can you place a hand there and acknowledge, "*I see you. I feel you. You're trying to protect me, and I'm grateful.*"

Zelda Marsh

Chapter 10: The Science of Healing

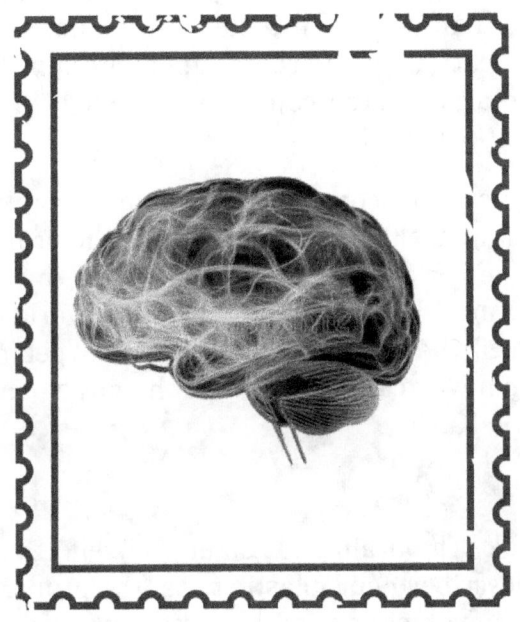

I Don't Need Your Forgiveness To Heal

The Bloody Miracle of Neuroplasticity

If you'd told me years ago that I could actually rewire my brain after trauma, I'd have laughed in your face. "Yeah, right," I'd have said. "And I suppose I can grow a third arm if I concentrate hard enough?" But the brain is more malleable than we give it credit for. It's not some fixed lump of meat that gets programmed once and then sits there like an outdated computer running Windows 95 for the rest of your life.

No, the brain is constantly changing, adapting, and reorganising itself. This ability is called neuroplasticity, and it's the reason I'm not still hiding in my bedroom with the curtains drawn, convinced the world is out to get me. Well, the world might still be out to get me, but at least I can now go to Tesco without having a panic attack in the cereal aisle.

In his book "The Brain That Changes Itself," Dr. Norman Doidge describes neuroplasticity as "the property of the brain that enables it to change its own structure and functioning in response to activity and mental experience." In other words, what you do and think changes your physical brain. Mind-blowing. Or should I say brain-changing?

When I first learned about neuroplasticity, I was sceptical. It sounded like one of those too-good-to-be-true concepts that wellness influencers bang on about while trying to sell you essential oils or crystals. "Just think positive thoughts, and your brain will rewire itself!" Yeah, and I'll grow wings and fly to the bloody moon while I'm at it.

But the science behind neuroplasticity is actually solid. Brain imaging studies have shown that the brain physically changes in response to experience. New neural connections form, unused ones wither away, and entire networks can be reorganised. It's like your brain is constantly under construction, with little neurological builders adding new roads, demolishing old buildings, and redirecting traffic.

For trauma survivors like me, this is incredibly hopeful news. It means that the neural pathways created during traumatic experiences, the ones that keep us stuck in hypervigilance, flashbacks, and maladaptive coping mechanisms, aren't permanent. They can be changed. We're not doomed to live with the brain that trauma built.

Of course, rewiring your brain isn't as simple as flipping a switch. It's more like trying to redirect a river that's been flowing the same way for decades. It takes time, consistent effort, and usually a fair bit of swearing. But it is possible. And that possibility keeps me going on days when healing feels like trying to climb Everest in flip-flops.

The Window of Tolerance: Or, Why I Sometimes Act Like a Complete Nutter

One of the most valuable concepts I've learned in my healing journey is the "window of tolerance," a term coined by Dr. Dan Siegel. It refers to the optimal zone of arousal where we can function effectively, not too hyped up or shut down. It's like Goldilocks if she were looking for the perfect state of nervous system regulation instead of porridge.

When we're within our window of tolerance, we can think clearly, feel our emotions without being overwhelmed, and respond to situations appropriately. We can handle stress without losing our shit or going numb. We can be present and engaged with life.

Trauma narrows this window considerably. Things that might be mildly stressful for someone else can send me rocketing out of my window of tolerance faster than you can say "fight-or-flight." One minute, I'm calmly discussing dinner plans, and the next, I'm either screaming about how nobody ever listens to me or completely dissociating. I am staring blankly at the wall, wondering if I've always been a wall-staring person or if this is a new development.

Understanding the window of tolerance helped me make sense of these seemingly random shifts in my behaviour and mood. I wasn't just being dramatic or oversensitive; my nervous system was what they call dysregulated due to trauma. My window of tolerance was so narrow that even small stressors could push me outside of it.

Zelda Marsh

The good news is that various practices and therapies can widen our window of tolerance. It's like stretching a muscle: the more you work at it, the more flexible it becomes. Through consistent practice, I've gradually expanded my capacity to stay regulated in the face of stress. I still have my moments (ask anyone who's seen me trying to assemble flat-pack furniture), but they're less frequent and intense than they used to be.

Dr. Siegel explains that expanding the window of tolerance involves developing the capacity to be aware of our internal states without being hijacked by them. He calls this "mindsight"—the ability to perceive our mind and the minds of others. It's like having an internal observer who can notice, "Oh, I'm starting to get triggered," without immediately being swept away by the trigger.

Developing this observer has been crucial for me. It's the difference between being completely identified with my trauma responses and having some perspective on them. It's the difference between "I am angry" and "I notice I'm feeling angry." That tiny bit of distance creates space for choice rather than automatic reaction.

Of course, developing this observer isn't easy when you've spent most of your life in survival mode. It's like trying to train a hypervigilant guard dog to chill out and give a polite woof instead of going full Cujo every time the doorbell rings. It takes patience, consistency, and a lot of treats. (In my case, the treats are cups of tea and the occasional biscuit. I'm easily bribed.)

The Polyvagal Theory: Or, Why I'm Not Just Being a Drama Queen

If you've ever wondered why you can't just "think positive" your way out of trauma responses, the Polyvagal Theory has your answer. Developed by Dr. Stephen Porges, this theory explains how our autonomic nervous system responds to safety and danger in largely unconscious and automatic ways.

The vagus nerve is the longest cranial nerve in the body, connecting the brain to various organs, including the heart, lungs, and digestive system. It's like the body's information superhighway,

carrying messages back and forth between brain and body. The Polyvagal Theory focuses on different branches of this nerve and how they relate to our stress responses.

According to Porges, we have three central autonomic states:

1. **Ventral Vagal** (social engagement): This is our "safe and social" state. We feel calm, connected, and capable of engaging with others when we're here. Our heart rate is regulated, our breathing is easy, and our digestion works properly. This is the state where healing, learning, and connecting happen. It's like being at a lovely dinner party where everyone's having a grand time, the food is delicious, and nobody's brought up politics.
2. **Sympathetic** (mobilisation): This is our "fight or flight" state. When we perceive danger, our sympathetic nervous system activates, increasing our heart rate, sending blood to our muscles, and

preparing us to fight or flee. This is useful in dangerous situations, but problematic when it becomes our default state. It's like being at a dinner party where someone's just flipped the table, and you're deciding whether to start throwing punches or make a run for it.

3. **Dorsal Vagal** (immobilisation): This is our "freeze" state, our most primitive response to life-threatening danger. Heart rate drops, breathing becomes shallow, and we might feel numb, disconnected, or "not really here." This is the body's last-ditch survival strategy when fighting or fleeing isn't an option. It's like being at a dinner party that's so unbearable you've mentally checked out and are now floating somewhere near the ceiling, watching yourself nod politely while thinking about what's on the telly later.

For those of us with trauma, our nervous system often gets stuck in sympathetic or dorsal vagal states, perceiving danger even in "safe" situations. We might be physically safe at a friend's birthday party, but our nervous system responds as if a lion across the Serengeti is chasing us. No wonder social events are so bloody exhausting.

Understanding the Polyvagal Theory helped me recognise these states and develop strategies for moving back toward the ventral vagus when I get dysregulated. It also helped me be less judgmental of my reactions. I wasn't being "too sensitive" or "overreacting"; my nervous system was doing exactly what it was designed to do based on its perception of threat. The problem wasn't the response itself but the faulty threat detection system that trauma had created.

Dr. Porges emphasises that our nervous system constantly evaluates risk in our environment through a process he calls "neuroception." This happens below the level of conscious awareness, which is why we can't just talk ourselves out of trauma responses. You can't reason with a nervous system that's convinced you're about to be eaten by a tiger, no matter how eloquent your arguments.

This explained why all my attempts at positive thinking and self-talk had limited effect on my trauma symptoms. I was trying to use my prefrontal cortex (the thinking part of my brain) to override responses happening in my limbic system and brainstem (the more primitive parts of my brain). It was like trying to stop a runaway train by standing in front of it and politely asking it to slow down. It is not very effective and will likely get you flattened.

The Triune Brain: Or, Why My Rational Mind and Emotional Mind Don't Talk to Each Other

Another helpful model for understanding trauma responses is the concept of the "triune brain," developed by neuroscientist Paul MacLean. While modern neuroscience has somewhat simplified and updated this model, it still offers a valuable framework for understanding how different parts of our brain respond to threats.

According to this model, our brain has three main parts that evolved at different times:

1. **The Reptilian Brain** (brainstem and cerebellum): This is the oldest part of our brain and is responsible for basic survival functions like breathing, heart rate, and body temperature. It's

concerned with physical survival and operates largely unconsciously. It's like the security guard of your brain, constantly monitoring for threats and ready to hit the panic button at a moment's notice.
2. **The Limbic System** (amygdala, hippocampus, hypothalamus): This is the emotional centre of our brain, involved in emotions, memory, and learning. It's particularly active in processing fear and plays a key role in trauma responses. It's like the drama queen of your brain, prone to emotional outbursts and holding grudges for things that happened decades ago.
3. **The Neocortex** (cerebral cortex): This is the newest part of our brain, responsible for higher-order functions like reasoning, language, and conscious thought. It makes us human and allows us to reflect on our experiences. It's like the professor of your brain, constantly analysing, planning, and trying to make sense of things.

In everyday life, these three brain parts work together relatively harmoniously. But trauma disrupts this harmony, causing the reptilian brain and limbic system to override the Neocortex in situations that trigger memories of past danger. This is why trauma survivors often find themselves reacting in ways that they know, intellectually, are not helpful or appropriate. The thinking brain gets hijacked by the survival brain.

I experienced this disconnect constantly before I began healing. I'd know, rationally, that I was safe at a friend's house, but my body would be in full fight-or-flight mode, heart racing, palms sweating, ready to bolt at the slightest provocation. My Neocortex would say, "This is ridiculous; you're just having dinner with friends," while my limbic system and reptilian brain screamed, "DANGER! ESCAPE NOW!"

Dr. Bessel van der Kolk describes this phenomenon in "The Body Keeps the Score," explaining that trauma causes a fundamental reorganisation of the way the mind and brain manage perceptions. He writes, "We have learned that trauma is not just an event that took place sometime in the past; it is also the imprint left by that experience on mind, brain, and body."

This affects how the different parts of our brain communicate. In trauma survivors, the amygdala (part of the limbic system responsible for detecting threats) becomes hyperactive. In contrast, the prefrontal cortex (part of the Neocortex responsible for rational thought) becomes less effective at regulating emotional responses.

It's like having an overly sensitive fire alarm that goes off when someone lights a candle and a sprinkler system that floods the entire building in response. Meanwhile, the building manager (your prefrontal cortex), who should be able to override the system and say, "It's just a candle; calm down," is locked out of the control room.

Understanding this brain dysfunction helped me be more compassionate with myself when I reacted in ways that seemed irrational. It wasn't that I was crazy or weak; it was that my brain had been rewired by trauma to prioritise survival over everything else. While this rewiring had once been adaptive, it had kept me alive during dangerous situations and was now getting in the way of living my whole life.

Zelda Marsh

The Trauma Timeline: Or, Why I'm Still Reacting to Things That Happened Decades Ago

One of the most confusing aspects of trauma is the way it collapses time. Events that happened years or even decades ago can feel as immediate and threatening as if they were happening now. This is because trauma disrupts the brain's normal processing of memory.

Dr. Francine Shapiro, the developer of EMDR (Eye Movement Desensitisation and Reprocessing) therapy, explains that traumatic memories are stored differently than ordinary memories. While normal memories are processed and integrated into our life narrative, traumatic memories often remain unprocessed, stored in their original, emotionally charged form.

This is why a trauma trigger can catapult us back in time, making us feel and react as if the traumatic event is happening in the present. We are not just remembering the past but reliving it with all the physical sensations, emotions, and beliefs present during the original event.

I experienced this time collapse regularly before I began healing. A certain tone of voice, phrase, or even a specific smell could instantly transport me back to traumatic childhood or early adulthood moments. In those moments, I wasn't a grown woman with agency and resources; I was a helpless child or a vulnerable young adult, experiencing the same fear, shame, and powerlessness I had felt then.

Dr. van der Kolk describes this phenomenon as "speechless terror", the way trauma can activate the brain's alarm system without engaging the parts of the brain responsible for language and time awareness. When this happens, we experience the emotional and physical components of the traumatic memory without the contextualising awareness that it happened in the past.

This explained why logical reassurances like "that was then, this is now" had little effect on my trauma responses. In those moments of triggering, my brain wasn't processing time normally. The past wasn't past but present, immediate, and threatening.

Once I understood that my time of collapse was crucial for my healing, it helped me recognise when I was being triggered and develop strategies for returning to the present moment. Grounding techniques that engaged my senses, such as feeling my feet on the floor, naming objects I could see, and holding something cold, helped anchor me in the here and now rather than being swept away by traumatic memories.

It also helped me understand why certain therapeutic approaches were more effective than others for trauma. Therapies that work directly with the body and nervous system, like EMDR, Somatic Experiencing, and sensorimotor psychotherapy, are often more effective for trauma than traditional talk therapy alone. These approaches help process traumatic memories so they can be integrated into our life narrative rather than remaining stuck in this timeless, unprocessed state.

Zelda Marsh

The Healing Brain: Or, How I Stopped Worrying and Learned to Love My Amygdala

Despite all the ways trauma disrupts the brain, the same neuroplasticity that allows trauma to rewire our brain also allows us to heal. The brain can change in response to any new experiences, new learning, and new patterns of thinking and behaving.

Dr Rick Hanson, a neuropsychologist and author of "Hardwiring Happiness," explains that we can actually use our mind to change our brain to change our mind. By deliberately cultivating positive experiences and mental states, we can create new neural pathways supporting well-being rather than distress.

This doesn't mean ignoring or suppressing negative experiences. It means balancing them with positive ones and learning to hold both with awareness and compassion. It's about expanding our capacity to experience the full range of human emotions without being overwhelmed.

For me, healing has involved a combination of approaches that work with different parts of my brain:

1. **Bottom-up approaches** that work with the reptilian brain and limbic system include somatic practices like yoga, breathwork, and movement that help regulate the nervous system. They also include therapies like EMDR and Somatic Experiencing that work directly with traumatic memories stored in the body.
2. **Top-down approaches** that work with the Neocortex: These include cognitive-behavioural therapy, mindfulness practices, and

psychoeducation that help me understand my trauma responses and develop new ways of thinking about my experiences.
3. **Relational approaches** that work with the social engagement system include secure therapeutic relationships, supportive friendships, and community connections that help rewire my brain's expectations about relationships.

Dr Daniel Siegel describes this integrated approach as "mindsight": the ability to perceive the mind (both our own and others) with clarity and compassion. He emphasises that healing involves integrating the different parts of ourselves, including the parts that carry trauma, rather than trying to get rid of them or fight against them.

This integration has been a key part of my healing journey. Rather than seeing my trauma responses as enemies to be conquered, I've learned to view them as protective parts that need to be acknowledged, understood, and gently guided toward new ways of keeping me safe.

For example, my tendency to people-please and abandon my own needs (the "fawn" response) developed as a way to stay safe in relationships where expressing my authentic self led to rejection or punishment. Rather than berating myself for this pattern, I've learned to thank this part of me for keeping me safe while helping it recognise that I now have other options for navigating relationships.

This compassionate approach to healing aligns with Internal Family Systems therapy, developed by Dr. Richard Schwartz. This model views the mind as naturally multiple, composed of sub-personalities or "parts" that can become extreme or dysfunctional when impacted by trauma. Healing involves developing a relationship with these parts from a place of curiosity and compassion rather than judgment or rejection.

The Science of Self-Compassion: OR Why Being Kind to Myself Isn't Just New Age Bollocks

One of the most powerful tools in healing trauma is self-compassion; the practice of treating ourselves with the same kindness and understanding we would give to a good friend. And before you roll your eyes and dismiss this as some hippy-dippy nonsense, let me tell you that there's solid science behind it.

Dr Kristin Neff, a pioneer in self-compassion research, has found that self-compassion is associated with greater emotional resilience, more accurate self-concepts, more caring relationship behaviour, and less narcissism and reactive anger. It's not about letting yourself off the hook or making excuses for bad behaviour; it's about relating to yourself with kindness rather than harsh criticism.

For trauma survivors, self-compassion can be particularly challenging. Many of us have internalised messages that we're fundamentally flawed, unworthy, or to blame for what happened to us. We often have a harsh inner critic that constantly berates us for our perceived failings and weaknesses.

I certainly did. My inner critic was like a particularly nasty schoolteacher, always ready to point out my mistakes and tell me I wasn't good enough. "You're too sensitive," it would say. "You're overreacting. Why can't you get over it? Everyone else has moved on. What's wrong with you?"

Learning to counter this critical voice with self-compassion was a game-changer for me. Instead of berating myself for my trauma responses, I began to acknowledge them with kindness. "Of course, you're feeling triggered right now," I would tell myself. "You've been through a lot, and your nervous system is trying to protect you. It's not your fault, and you're doing your best."

This shift from self-criticism to self-compassion didn't happen overnight; it wasn't always easy. There were (and still are) days when my inner critic was particularly loud and persistent. But with practice, I've developed a stronger self-compassionate voice that can counter the criticism and offer a more balanced perspective.

Dr. Neff identifies three components of self-compassion:

1. **Self-kindness vs. Self-judgment**: Being gentle and understanding with ourselves rather than harshly critical.
2. **Common humanity vs. Isolation**: Recognising that suffering is part of the shared human experience rather than feeling isolated by our struggles.
3. **Mindfulness vs. Over-Identification**: Holding our painful thoughts and feelings in balanced awareness rather than over-identifying with them.

These components work together to create a more supportive relationship with ourselves, which is essential for healing trauma. When we're constantly at war with ourselves, criticising our responses and pushing away our pain, we create additional suffering on top of the trauma itself. It's like having a broken leg and then beating yourself up for not being able to run a marathon. And for someone who broke her femur and snapped in two, because she thought she was **She-Ra** and tried to carry a bloody cabin bed down the stairs by herself, know this is impossible.

Self-compassion creates a safe internal environment where healing can occur. It's like building a secure base within ourselves, a place of acceptance and understanding from which we can explore our trauma without being overwhelmed by it.

Research supports this idea. Studies have found that self-compassion is associated with lower levels of anxiety, depression, and PTSD symptoms. It's also linked to greater emotional regulation abilities, which are often compromised in trauma survivors.

Dr Christopher Germer, a clinical psychologist and mindfulness teacher, describes self-compassion as "a form of acceptance: acceptance of ourselves and our experience at the moment, especially when we're suffering." This acceptance doesn't mean resignation or giving up on change; instead, it creates the conditions under which change becomes possible.

Self-compassion has been both a practice and a path for me. I cultivate it daily through formal practices like loving-kindness meditation and informal practices like speaking to myself with kindness throughout the day. It's a path that leads toward greater healing, resilience, and wholeness.

The Neuroscience of Connection: Or, Why I Can't Heal in Isolation No Matter How Much I Want To

As much as I sometimes wish I could heal all by myself (preferably while hiding under a duvet with a cup of tea and a good book), the science is clear: human connection is essential for healing trauma. Our brains are wired for connection, and healthy relationships play a crucial role in rewiring the neural pathways disrupted by trauma.

Dr. Bruce Perry, a psychiatrist and neuroscientist, emphasises that "the brain is a social organ, made to be in relationships." He explains that our brains develop in the context of relationships and heal in the context of relationships, too.

This makes sense from an evolutionary perspective. Humans are social animals who have survived by cooperating and living in groups. Our nervous systems are designed to regulate in connection with others, a process called "co-regulation." When we're with someone calm and regulated, our nervous system tends to synchronise with theirs, moving toward regulation as well.

For trauma survivors, this co-regulation is particularly important because our self-regulation capacities have often been compromised by trauma. We may struggle to calm our nervous system on our own, but in the presence of a regulated other, our system can begin to remember what regulation feels like.

This explained why isolation always made my symptoms worse. Without the co-regulating presence of others, my nervous system had no external reference point for safety, no model for regulation. I was stuck in my own dysregulated patterns with no way to break free.

Dr Stephen Porges' Polyvagal Theory, which we discussed earlier, includes the concept of the "social engagement system", a network of nerves that connects our brain to our face, voice, and heart, allowing us to communicate and connect with others. This system plays a crucial role in regulating our nervous system and helping us feel safe.

When we're in a ventral vagal state (our "safe and social" state), our social engagement system is online, allowing us to connect with others, read social cues, and engage in reciprocal communication. But when we're in sympathetic arousal (fight/flight) or dorsal vagal collapse (freeze), this system goes offline, making it difficult to connect with others meaningfully.

This created a catch-22 for me: I needed a connection to heal, but my dysregulated nervous system made it difficult to connect. I would isolate when I was struggling, which would make my symptoms worse, which would make me isolate more, creating a downward spiral of disconnection and dysregulation.

Breaking this cycle involved gradually building connections with people who could meet me where I was and offer co-regulation without demanding that I be "fine" or "over it." This included therapists, support groups, and friends who understood trauma and could hold space for my experiences without judgment or pressure to "just move on."

Dr. Gabor Maté emphasises that "trauma is not what happens to you, but what happens inside you as a result of what happened to you." And what happens inside us is a profound disconnection from ourselves, others, and our innate capacity for well-being. Healing, then, involves reconnection on all these levels.

This reconnection isn't always easy. Trauma often leaves us with deep fears about relationships, beliefs that we're unworthy of connection, or patterns of relating that push others away even as we long for closeness. Working through these barriers to connection has been some of my healing journey's most challenging and rewarding work.

The Body Keeps the Score: OR Why Talking About Trauma Isn't Enough

One of the most significant advances in trauma treatment is the recognition that trauma is stored in the body, not just the mind. Dr. Bessel van der Kolk's groundbreaking book, "The Body Keeps the Score," brought this concept into mainstream awareness. Still, many cultures and healing traditions have recognised this bodily dimension of trauma for centuries.

Trauma impacts our entire organism, thoughts, emotions, physical sensations, and behaviours. It imprints on our nervous system, muscles, posture, and movement. This is why purely cognitive approaches to healing trauma often fall short. You can't talk your way out of something stored in your body.

Zelda Marsh

I discovered this the hard way. I spent years in traditional talk therapy, analysing my past, understanding the origins of my patterns, and developing insights about my trauma. And while this was valuable, it helped me make sense of my experiences and develop compassion for myself, it didn't resolve the physical symptoms of trauma. I still experienced panic attacks, chronic tension, digestive issues, and a persistent sense of being unsafe in my body.

It wasn't until I began working with body-centred approaches that I started to experience more profound healing. Practices like yoga, breathwork, and somatic experiencing helped me reconnect with my body, release stored tension, and develop a greater sense of safety and agency in my physical self.

Dr. Peter Levine, the developer of Somatic Experiencing, explains that trauma is primarily about the nervous system's response to overwhelming events, not the events themselves. When we can't complete the natural defensive responses to threats (fight, flight, or freeze), the energy of those responses gets trapped in our body, creating symptoms of trauma.

Healing involves completing these incomplete responses and discharging the trapped energy. This might look like trembling, shaking, crying, or expressing anger in a safe and contained way. It's about allowing the body to do what it couldn't do during the traumatic event, to move through the defensive response and return to a state of regulation.

This somatic dimension of healing was both challenging and liberating for me. It was challenging because it meant facing sensations and emotions that I'd spent years avoiding or suppressing. It was liberating because it offered a path to healing that didn't depend solely on understanding or insight but on direct experience and embodied change.

Dr. Pat Ogden, the founder of Sensorimotor Psychotherapy, emphasises the importance of healing trauma with the body's wisdom. She explains that the body often knows what it needs to heal before the conscious mind does. By paying attention to physical sensations, impulses, and movements, we can access this bodily wisdom and allow it to guide our healing process.

This has involved learning to listen to my body's signals rather than overriding them with my mind. It meant honouring my physical boundaries, respecting my body's need for rest and regulation, and allowing self-expression that feels authentic rather than forced.

This body-centred approach to healing aligns with emerging research on the neurobiology of trauma. Studies using brain imaging techniques have shown that trauma impacts areas of the brain involved in bodily awareness, emotional regulation, and the sense of self. Healing these impacts requires approaches that work directly with the body and nervous system, not just with thoughts and beliefs.

The Integration of Healing Modalities: Or, Why There's No One-Size-Fits-All Approach

One of the most important things I've learned in my healing journey is that no single approach works for everyone. Healing trauma is a highly individual process that often requires a combination of modalities tailored to your specific needs, history, and preferences.

Dr. Judith Herman, a pioneer in trauma research and treatment, describes trauma recovery as occurring in three stages: establishing safety, remembering and mourning, and reconnection with ordinary life. Different approaches may be more helpful at different stages of this process.

For example, when safety is the primary concern in the early stages of healing, approaches focusing on nervous system regulation and building resources may be most helpful. These might include:

- Somatic practices like yoga, tai chi, or qigong
- Mindfulness and meditation practices
- Breathwork and other autonomic nervous system regulators
- Lifestyle changes that support physical well-being
- Building a support network of safe relationships

As safety is established, approaches that help process traumatic memories may become more appropriate. These might include:

- EMDR (Eye Movement Desensitisation and Reprocessing)
- Somatic Experiencing
- Internal Family Systems therapy
- Narrative therapy
- Art therapy or other expressive approaches

In the later stages of healing, as you reconnect with life and build a new sense of self and purpose, approaches that focus on growth and meaning may be most relevant. These might include:

- Existential therapy
- Post-traumatic growth frameworks
- Community involvement and activism
- Creative expression and meaning-making
- Spiritual or philosophical exploration

My healing journey has included elements from all these categories, sometimes simultaneously and sometimes sequentially. I've worked with traditional talk therapy, EMDR, somatic experiencing, yoga, meditation, breathwork, internal family systems, and various creative and expressive approaches.

What's been most helpful has shifted as my needs and capacities have changed. In the early stages, when I was frequently overwhelmed and dysregulated, approaches focused on safety and regulation were most important. As I developed more stability, I was able to engage with approaches that involved processing traumatic memories without becoming overwhelmed.

Dr Janina Fisher, a trauma specialist and author, emphasises the importance of this phased approach to trauma treatment. She cautions against diving into trauma processing before sufficient safety and regulation skills have been established, as this can lead to re-traumatisation rather than healing.

This phased approach doesn't mean healing is a linear process with clear-cut stages. It's more like a spiral, where we revisit similar themes at deeper levels as we heal. Even if we've done significant trauma processing work, we might need to return to focusing on safety and regulation during particularly stressful periods.

The key is to honour your own pace and needs rather than forcing yourself into approaches that don't feel right or overwhelm your current capacities. Healing isn't a race or a competition; it's a deeply personal journey that unfolds in its own time and way.

The Science of Post-Traumatic Growth: Or, How I Found Gifts in the Garbage

One of the most hopeful aspects of trauma research is the concept of post-traumatic growth: the idea that people can experience positive psychological changes as a result of struggling with ridiculously high challenges and life's circumstances. This doesn't mean that trauma is a good thing or that we should be grateful for traumatic experiences. Instead, it recognises that in the process of healing from trauma, many people discover strengths, insights, and capacities they might not have developed otherwise.

Dr. Richard Tedeschi and Dr. Lawrence Calhoun, the psychologists who first coined the term "post-traumatic growth," identify five areas where this growth commonly occurs:

1. **Greater appreciation of life and changed priorities**: Many trauma survivors report a deeper appreciation for life and a shift in what they value most.
2. **Warmer, more intimate relationships**: Many survivors develop greater compassion for others

and a deeper capacity for connection after facing suffering.
3. **Greater sense of personal strength**: Surviving trauma could lead to the realisation, "If I lived through that, I could face anything."
4. **Recognition of new possibilities or paths for one's life**: Trauma often disrupts our expected life path, opening up new directions we might not have considered otherwise.
5. **Spiritual development**: Many survivors report deeper spiritual connections or more meaningful engagement with existential questions.

Through my healing journey, I've experienced growth in all these areas. I have a much deeper appreciation for simple joys and everyday beauty. I've developed more authentic, vulnerable relationships based on genuine connection rather than people-pleasing or performance. I've discovered strengths and capacities I never knew I had. I've found a new purpose in sharing my healing journey and supporting others on theirs. And I've developed a more meaningful spiritual practice that honours my authentic experience rather than conforming to external expectations.

This growth didn't happen automatically or easily. It emerged through the deliberate work of healing, through facing my pain rather than avoiding it, through making meaning of my experiences rather than being defined by them. And it doesn't erase or justify the trauma itself. I would still prefer not to have experienced trauma, but given that I did, I'm grateful for the growth that has come through healing it.

Zelda Marsh

Dr Tedeschi emphasises that post-traumatic growth isn't about returning to who you were before the trauma but about being transformed by your experiences in positive ways. It's not about "getting over it" but about integrating the trauma into your life narrative in a way that allows for new meaning and purpose.

This concept of growth through adversity isn't new. Many spiritual and philosophical traditions recognise that suffering, while not desirable in itself, can be a catalyst for profound transformation. What's new is the scientific research validating this ancient wisdom and identifying the factors that promote growth rather than just distress after trauma.

One key factor is narrative development—the ability to create a coherent story about your experiences that acknowledges the pain of trauma and the possibility of growth. This doesn't mean creating a simplistic "silver lining" narrative that minimises suffering. Rather, it means developing a complex, nuanced understanding of how trauma has impacted you and how you've responded to that impact.

Another factor is social support, which is having relationships where you can process your experiences without judgment or pressure to "just move on." Research has found that supportive relationships are one of the strongest predictors of post-traumatic growth.

A third factor is finding meaning in suffering, not in the sense that the trauma itself was meaningful or purposeful, but in the sense that your response to it can create meaning and purpose. This might involve using your experiences to help others, advocating for change, or developing greater compassion for yourself and others who suffer.

I Don't Need Your Forgiveness To Heal

Writing this book is part of my post-traumatic growth. It's a way of making meaning from my experiences and using what I've learned to help others heal. I'm not grateful for the trauma itself, but I am thankful for what I've discovered through healing it—about myself, about resilience, about the capacity for growth even in the darkest circumstances.

Zelda Marsh

The Ongoing Journey: Or, Why Healing Isn't a Destination but a Way of Life

One of the most important things I've learned about trauma healing is that it's not a linear process with a clear endpoint. It's more like a spiral, where we revisit similar themes at deeper levels as we grow and change. It's not about reaching some perfect state of healing where we never struggle again; it's about developing the capacity to work with our struggles more skilfully and compassionately.

Dr. Judith Herman describes trauma recovery as a process of "remembering and mourning" rather than "forgetting and moving on." We don't erase the trauma from our history; we integrate it into our life narrative in a way that allows us to move forward without being defined or limited by it.

This ongoing nature of healing can be frustrating at times. Just when I think I've "dealt with" a particular aspect of my trauma, it shows up again in a new form or context. But I've seen these recurrences not as failures or setbacks but as opportunities to heal at deeper levels, to bring more awareness and compassion to parts of myself that still carry wounds.

Dr. Peter Levine describes this process using the metaphor of a pendulum. Healing involves swinging between activation (engaging with traumatic material) and resourcing (connecting with safety and regulation). Over time, the pendulum swings become less extreme as we develop a greater capacity to hold both activation and regulation simultaneously.

This pendulum metaphor has helped me normalise the ups and downs of healing. When I feel triggered or overwhelmed, I remind myself this is just one swing of the pendulum, not a sign that all my healing work has been for nothing. I focus on resourcing and connecting with practices and relationships that help me return to regulation.

Dr Janina Fisher emphasises that healing isn't about eliminating trauma responses but about expanding our window of tolerance so that we have more options for responding to triggers. We develop the capacity to notice when we're being triggered without automatically reacting from that triggered place. We learn to hold our trauma responses with awareness and compassion rather than being completely identified with them.

This expanded capacity has been one of the most significant changes in my healing journey. I still get triggered, probably always will to some extent, but I'm no longer at the mercy of my triggers. I can notice them, name them, and choose how to respond rather than reacting automatically. I can hold the triggered part of me with compassion while maintaining a connection with my adult self. Who knows, I'm safe now.

Dr. Dan Siegel describes this capacity as "mindsight", the ability to perceive our mind with clarity and compassion. It's like developing an internal observer who can witness our experiences without being completely swept away.

Zelda Marsh

This observer creates space between stimulus and response, between trigger and reaction, allowing for choice rather than automatic behaviour.

Developing this observer has been crucial for my healing. It's the difference between "I am angry" and "I notice I'm feeling angry." That tiny bit of distance creates space for choice rather than automatic reaction. It allows me to respond to situations based on what's happening now rather than being driven by past trauma.

This doesn't mean I never react from a triggered place. I'm human, and healing is an ongoing process. But when I react in ways that don't align with my values or intentions, I can recognise it sooner, repair any harm caused, and learn from the experience rather than spiral into shame or self-criticism.

Dr Kristin Neff's research on self-compassion shows that this accepting relationship with ourselves is more motivating for positive change than harsh self-criticism. When we beat ourselves up for our mistakes or struggles, we activate the threat system in our brains, making it harder to learn and grow. When we approach ourselves with compassion, we create the conditions under which change becomes possible.

This self-compassionate approach to healing has been transformative for me. Instead of seeing healing as a linear path that I should be further along, I've come to view it as a cyclical process of growth, challenge, integration, and renewal. Each cycle brings new insights, capacities, and opportunities for deeper healing.

And perhaps most importantly, I've learned that healing isn't just about reducing symptoms or resolving past trauma. It's about creating a life worth living, characterised by presence, connection, meaning, and joy. It's about surviving and thriving, not just existing but fully living.

This doesn't mean every day is wonderful or that I never struggle. Life still has its challenges, and I still have my wounds. But I'm no longer defined or limited by those wounds. They're part of my story but not the whole story. And that is the accurate measure of healing; not that the wounds disappear, but that they no longer determine the shape and scope of our lives.

Zelda Marsh

Chapter 11: Forgiveness vs Freedom

Let's talk about the F-word.

No, not that one, though I'm rather fond of it, and I'll bet your last quid that you expected many more F bombs in this book! I'm talking about Forgiveness, that sacred cow of healing that everyone from your grandma to Oprah will tell you is essential for moving on.

"You must forgive to heal." "Forgiveness sets you free." "Holding onto anger is like drinking poison and expecting the other person to die."

We've all heard these platitudes. They're stitched into cushions, printed on mugs, and plastered across Instagram in swirly fonts over sunset backgrounds. They're delivered by well-meaning friends, therapists, spiritual leaders, and random blokes down the pub who suddenly fancy themselves life coaches after three pints.

And they're effing bollocks.

At least, they're bollocks when they're forced on trauma survivors as the only path to healing.

The Forgiveness Industrial Complex

There's an entire industry built around Forgiveness. Books, workshops, retreats, and online courses promise that you'll finally be free if you forgive those who hurt you.

It's a seductive promise. Who doesn't want freedom from pain? Who doesn't want to move on from trauma? Who doesn't want to feel lighter, happier, and more at peace?

But they don't tell you that Forgiveness isn't the only path to healing. For many trauma survivors, it's not even a helpful path. And when it's pushed as a moral imperative rather than a personal choice, it can actually re-traumatise.

Dr. Judith Herman, a pioneering researcher in trauma recovery, points out that the pressure to forgive often serves the needs of the perpetrator or the community more than the survivor. It's saying, "Hurry up and get over it so we can all move on and not have to deal with your messy feelings anymore."

This pressure is particularly intense for women, who are socialised to prioritise harmony over justice and relationships over self-protection. We're taught that being "good" means forgiving, regardless of whether the person who harmed us has acknowledged the harm, taken responsibility, or changed their behaviour.

But what if Forgiveness isn't what you need?

What if what you need is anger?

Boundaries?

Justice?

Distance?

What if you need to prioritise your own healing over everyone else's comfort, finally?

The Toxic Forgiveness Trap

Let me tell you about my own journey with the F-word. For years, I tried to forgive. I really did. I journaled about it. Prayed about it. Meditated on it and tried to find compassion for those who had hurt me.

"They did the best they could with what they had." "They were wounded themselves." "They didn't know any better."

I repeated these mantras like magic spells that would finally free me from pain. And sometimes, briefly, they worked. I'd feel a momentary sense of peace, of release.

But it never lasted. Deep down, my body knew something my mind was trying to deny: some things are unforgivable. Not because I'm vindictive or hold grudges, but because some violations cut so deep that Forgiveness feels like another form of self-betrayal.

The twelve-year-old boy who raped me? Maybe he was a victim himself. Perhaps he was acting out his own trauma. Maybe he didn't fully understand the impact of his actions.

But you know what? That doesn't make what he did okay. It doesn't erase the decades of pain I've carried. It doesn't give him the right to my Forgiveness.

My mother, who exposed my violation to her friends instead of protecting me, and then shamed me into silence? Maybe she was overwhelmed. Perhaps she didn't know how to handle it. Maybe she was doing the best she could.

But her "best" wasn't good enough. Her "best" left me with shame that wasn't mine. Her "best" taught me that my pain wasn't important, that my boundaries didn't matter, that my voice wouldn't be heard.

Zelda Marsh

The partners who betrayed me, who used my trauma history against me, who gaslit me into believing I was "too much" or "too sensitive"? Maybe they had their own issues. Perhaps they weren't equipped for a relationship with someone with complex trauma. Maybe they didn't intend to cause harm.

But intention doesn't erase impact. Their actions still hurt, their betrayals still left scars, and their gaslighting made me doubt my reality.

Trying to force Forgiveness for these violations felt like violence against myself. It felt like saying, "What happened to you doesn't matter. Your pain isn't that important. Just get over it already."

And that's the toxic forgiveness trap: when the pressure to forgive becomes another form of silencing, another way of minimising trauma, another burden for survivors to bear.

The Freedom of Boundaries

What actually helped me heal wasn't Forgiveness. It was boundaries.

Clear, firm, unapologetic boundaries about what I would and wouldn't accept. About who got access to me and who didn't. About how I would and wouldn't be treated.

Dr Harriet Lerner, author of The Dance of Anger, defines boundaries as "the limits we set with other people, which indicate what we find acceptable and unacceptable in their behaviour toward us."

For trauma survivors, especially those who experienced boundary violations in childhood, setting boundaries can feel impossible. We've been conditioned to believe that our needs don't matter, that saying "no" is dangerous and that prioritising our own wellbeing is selfish.

But boundaries aren't selfish, they're essential. They're not about punishing others; they're about protecting ourselves. They're not walls but filters that let in what's healthy and keep out what's harmful.

For me, setting boundaries looked like this:

Cutting contact with family members who continued to deny or minimise my trauma. Ending relationships with partners who couldn't respect my healing process. Walking away from friendships that drained rather than supported me. Saying "no" to social obligations felt overwhelming. Limiting my exposure to people, places, and situations that triggered my trauma responses.

These boundaries weren't about revenge or holding grudges. They were about creating physical, emotional, and psychological safety for genuine healing.

And here's what I discovered: boundaries are more freeing than Forgiveness. While Forgiveness requires you to somehow make peace with what happened, boundaries allow you to create a life where those violations can't happen again.

The Self-Forgiveness Revolution

While I've struggled with forgiving others, there is one person I've had to learn to forgive: myself.

For staying in abusive relationships too long. For not protecting my younger self. For these reasons, I abandoned my own needs to please others. For the times I ignored my body's wisdom. For believing I deserved less than love, respect, and safety.

This kind of self-forgiveness isn't about letting myself off the hook or avoiding responsibility. It's about recognising that I was doing the best I could with the tools I had at the time. Many of my "mistakes" were actually trauma response adaptations that helped me survive in unsafe environments.

Dr. Kristin Neff, a leading researcher on self-compassion, distinguishes between self-esteem (based on positive evaluation) and self-compassion (based on kindness toward oneself regardless of perceived success or failure). Self-compassion, she argues, is more stable and more conducive to psychological well-being than self-esteem.

For trauma survivors, self-compassion can be revolutionary. We're often our own harshest critics, internalising the negative messages we receive from others. Learning to speak to ourselves with kindness rather than criticism, with understanding rather than judgment, can transform our relationship with ourselves and, by extension, our trauma.

This doesn't mean excusing harmful behaviours or avoiding accountability. It means holding ourselves accountable with compassion rather than shame. It means recognising that healing isn't linear, that setbacks aren't failures, and that we're allowed to be messy and imperfect as we navigate the complex terrain of trauma recovery.

For me, self-forgiveness has been a daily practice, a conscious choice to treat myself with the same kindness I would offer a friend, to recognise when I'm slipping into self-criticism or shame spirals, and to gently bring myself back to compassion.

It's not easy. The inner critic has had decades to perfect its script. But each time I choose self-compassion over self-judgment, I'm rewriting that script, creating new neural pathways, and teaching my nervous system that it's safe to be imperfect, to make mistakes, and to be human.

The Acceptance Alternative

If not Forgiveness, then what? How do we move forward from trauma without getting stuck in bitterness or resentment?

For me, the answer has been acceptance.

Not acceptance in the sense of saying what happened was okay, not acceptance as resignation or giving up, but acceptance as acknowledging reality precisely as it is, without denial, minimisation, or wishful thinking.

Acceptance means saying, **"This happened. It wasn't okay. It caused real harm. And it's part of my story, but doesn't define it."**

Acceptance means recognising that I can't change the past but can change how I relate to it. I can't undo the trauma, but I can heal from it. I can't make those who hurt me take responsibility, but I can take responsibility for my healing.

This kind of acceptance is actually more demanding than Forgiveness. It requires looking directly at what happened, feeling the full range of emotions it evokes, and still choosing to move forward. It requires grieving what was lost, what was taken, what never got to be.

But it's also more honest. It doesn't ask us to pretend we're okay with things that are fundamentally not okay. It doesn't require us to manufacture positive feelings toward those who harmed us. It simply asks us to acknowledge reality, not as we wish it were.

And from that place of honest acceptance, genuine healing becomes possible.

The Compassion Distinction

There's an important distinction: you can have compassion for someone without forgiving them.

Compassion means recognising the humanity in another person, even when they've acted inhumanely. It means understanding that hurt people hurt people and that most harmful behaviour comes from unhealed wounds.

The twelve-year-old boy and babysitters who raped me? I can have compassion for whatever circumstances led them to violate another child without excusing or minimising what he did. I can hope they got help, that they didn't go on to harm others, that they found healing for whatever drove them to cause harm.

My mother? I can have compassion for her own trauma history, for the limitations of her parenting skills, and for the cultural context that didn't equip her to handle sexual abuse appropriately. I can recognise that she was doing the best she could with the tools she had.

The partners who betrayed me? I can have compassion for their attachment wounds, fears, and limitations. I understand that their behaviour was more about their issues than my worth.

This compassion doesn't require me to maintain relationships with these people. It doesn't obligate me to trust them again. It doesn't mean I have to expose myself to potential further harm.

It simply means I recognise their humanity, even as I maintain my boundaries. It means I don't reduce them to monsters or villains in my story, even as I acknowledge the real harm they caused.

This distinction between compassion and Forgiveness has been crucial in my healing journey. It's allowed me to release anger and resentment, which is weighing me down, without forcing myself into a false forgiveness that doesn't feel authentic.

Zelda Marsh

The Freedom Beyond Forgiveness

Here's what I've discovered: there is freedom beyond Forgiveness. Freedom that doesn't require you to make peace with those who harmed you, freedom that doesn't ask you to minimise your trauma or silence your truth.

This freedom comes from reclaiming your narrative. It comes from recognising that while you can't control what happened to you, you can control how you integrate it into your life story. It comes from understanding that your worth isn't determined by what was done to you but by your inherent value as a human being.

It comes from creating a life that reflects your values, not your trauma. It comes from building relationships based on mutual respect and care, not reenactments of old wounds. It comes from making choices that honour your needs and boundaries, not perpetuating patterns of self-abandonment.

It comes from recognising that healing isn't about getting back to who you were before the trauma, it's about becoming who you were always meant to be, with the trauma as part of your journey but not the destination.

This freedom doesn't happen overnight. It's not a single decision or revelation. It's thousands of small choices, day after day, to prioritise your wellbeing, honour your truth, trust your body's wisdom, and surround yourself with people who respect your boundaries and support your healing.

Sometimes, it includes Forgiveness, when it feels right, serves your healing, and is freely chosen rather than imposed. But Forgiveness is never the prerequisite for freedom. It's just one possible path among many.

The Both/And Reality

One of the most liberating realisations in my healing journey has been embracing the **both/and** nature of trauma and recovery.

I can **Both** acknowledge the real harm done to me **AND** refuse to be defined by it. I can **both** have compassion for those who hurt me **AND** maintain firm boundaries with them. I can **both** grieve what I lost **AND** celebrate what I've built from the ashes. I can **both** honour the pain of my past **AND** create joy in my present. I can **both** recognise the ways trauma shaped me **AND** choose how I want to grow beyond it.

This **both/and** thinking is what psychologists call "dialectical thinking", the ability to hold seemingly contradictory truths simultaneously. It's a more nuanced, complex way of understanding reality than the either/or thinking that often dominates discussions of trauma and healing.

Either/or thinking says you must either forgive or remain bitter. Either move on completely or stay stuck in the past. Either demonise those who hurt you or excuse their behaviour.

Both/thinking allows for the messy, complicated reality of trauma recovery. It creates space for the full range of human experience: the grief and growth, the anger and compassion, the wounds and the wisdom.

And it's in this space, this honest, nuanced, **both/and** space, that true healing happens.

Zelda Marsh

Reflection: Your Relationship with Forgiveness

What's your relationship with Forgiveness? Has it been presented to you as the only path to healing? Have you felt pressured to forgive before you were ready or to forgive people who haven't acknowledged the harm they caused?

Forgiveness has been a genuine source of freedom for you. It could have been an essential part of your healing journey, freely chosen rather than imposed.

There's no right or wrong here, no universal prescription for healing. What matters is what's true for you. what serves your wellbeing, honours your experience, and creates genuine freedom rather than false peace.

The question isn't whether you should forgive. The question is: what do you need to heal? What boundaries would support your wellbeing? What would help you reclaim your power and agency? What would allow you to create a life that reflects your values rather than your wounds?

These are the questions worth asking. And only you can answer them.

Reflection Prompt: What does the word "forgiveness" bring up in your body?

Is there tension, resistance, or relief?

If Forgiveness has been difficult, what boundaries should you set instead?

I Don't Need Your Forgiveness To Heal

Where in your life might self-forgiveness be more important than forgiving others?

Zelda Marsh

Chapter 12: The Ongoing Journey

The Myth of "Getting Over It": Or, Why Healing Isn't a Bloody Finish Line

If there's one thing that makes me want to throw my tea mug across the room (and I'd never waste good tea, mind you), it's when someone asks if I'm "over" my trauma yet. As if trauma is some nasty cold you take paracetamol for, have a good kip, and wake up right as rain the next morning.

"**Are you over it yet**?" they ask, with that head-tilted look of concern that really means. "**It's been ages; shouldn't you be normal by now**?" I always want to respond, "Oh yes, completely over it. I took two 'Get Over Trauma' pills last Tuesday, and by Friday, I was brand new. I even got a certificate in the post saying, 'Congratulations! You're Healed! "

The truth is, healing from trauma isn't about "getting over it" or reaching some magical finish line where everything is sorted, and you never struggle again. It's more like learning to live with a wonky knee: some days, it barely bothers you; other days, it's giving you gyp, and you're always aware of which activities might set it off. But you learn to work with it rather than letting it stop you from living your life.

Dr. Judith Herman, one of the pioneers in trauma research, describes recovery as a process of "remembering and mourning" rather than "forgetting and moving on." We don't erase trauma from our history; we integrate it into our life narrative in a way that allows us to move forward without being defined or limited by it.

Zelda Marsh

This ongoing nature of healing can be bloody frustrating at times. Just when I think I've "dealt with" a particular aspect of my trauma, it shows up again in a new form or context. Like that annoying relative who keeps turning up at family gatherings even though nobody remembers inviting them. ***"Oh, hello, abandonment issues. Thought you'd buggered off years ago, but here you are again. Lovely."***

But I've seen these constant showups not as failures or setbacks but as opportunities to heal at deeper levels, to bring more awareness and compassion to parts of myself that still carry wounds. It's like peeling an onion, each layer reveals another underneath, and yes, sometimes it makes you cry, but it's all part of getting to the core.

Dr. Peter Levine uses the pendulum metaphor to describe this process. Healing involves swinging between activation (engaging with traumatic material) and resourcing (connecting with safety and regulation). Over time, the pendulum swings become less extreme as we develop a greater capacity to hold both activation and regulation simultaneously.

I prefer to think of it as learning to dance with my trauma rather than fighting against it or trying to outrun it. Some days, it's a graceful waltz; others, it's more like I'm being dragged around the dance floor by a drunken uncle at a wedding. But either way, I'm still dancing rather than sitting frozen on the sidelines.

The "Good Enough" Healing: Or, Why Perfectionism Can Sod Right Off

One of the most liberating moments in my healing journey was realising that I didn't need to be perfectly healed to have a good life. I didn't need to eradicate every trigger, resolve every issue, or transform every wound into some profound spiritual lesson. I just needed to be "good enough", functional enough to live a meaningful life aligned with my values.

This concept of "good enough" comes from the psychoanalyst D.W. Winnicott, who talked about the "good enough mother", not a perfect parent, but one who meets their child's needs adequately most of the time. Similarly, "good enough" healing doesn't mean ideal healing; it means healing that allows you to live your life without being dominated by trauma responses.

For me, "*good enough*" healing means:

- *I still get triggered sometimes, but I recover more quickly*
- *I have bad days, but they don't turn into bad weeks or months*
- *I can recognise when I'm in a trauma response rather than believing that's just "how I am."*
- *I have tools and practices that help me return to regulation when I get dysregulated*
- *I can maintain meaningful relationships even when they're challenging*
- *I can experience joy, pleasure, and connection without waiting for the other shoe to drop*
- *I can pursue goals and dreams without being paralysed by fear or shame*

Zelda Marsh

After years of perfectionism, this "good enough" approach has been a massive relief. I used to think I needed to be completely healed before I could really live my life. I was waiting to arrive at some mythical state of perfect mental health before allowing myself to pursue relationships, career goals, or even simple pleasures.

It was like saying, "I'll start living once I've sorted out all my issues", which, if you think about it, is a bit like saying, "I'll start swimming once I'm completely dry." It just doesn't work that way. We heal by living, not the other way around.

Dr Brené Brown talks about perfectionism as a form of armour: a way of protecting ourselves from vulnerability, judgment, and shame. For trauma survivors, perfectionism often becomes a strategy for trying to control an unpredictable world. If we can be perfect enough and do everything right, maybe we can prevent bad things from happening again.

I was the queen of this kind of thinking. If I could just be perfect, the perfect daughter, student, friend, partner, employee, maybe I could finally be safe. Perhaps I could finally be worthy of love and belonging. Maybe I could finally stop feeling like I was constantly walking on eggshells, waiting for the next disaster.

But perfectionism is an impossible standard that keeps us in shame and fear. It's like trying to climb a mountain that grows taller with every step. You never arrive; you get more exhausted.

Embracing "good enough" healing doesn't mean settling for less or giving up on growth. It means acknowledging that healing is a lifelong journey, not a destination and that we can live meaningful lives while still healing. It means recognising that we don't have to wait until we are healed to start living.

As the saying goes, "**We don't heal to live; we live to heal**." With all its messiness, challenges, joys, and connections, life itself is the context in which healing happens. We don't need to put life on hold until we're "**fixed**"; we need to engage with life as part of the fixing process.

This shift from perfectionism to "**good enough**" has been one of the most liberating aspects of my healing journey. It's allowed me to stop holding my breath, waiting for some perfect future state, and start living now, imperfections and all. It's allowed me to be human rather than superhuman, which is a relief because the cape was chafing.

The Boundaries Without Forgiveness: Or, How to Tell People to Sod Off Without Feeling Guilty

One of the most powerful tools in my healing toolkit has been learning to set and maintain boundaries without requiring Forgiveness as a prerequisite. This has been especially important in dealing with the people who hurt me or who continue to engage in harmful behaviours.

For years, I bought into the cultural narrative that setting boundaries with family members or cutting contact with abusive people was "mean" or "unforgiving." I felt guilty for protecting myself as if my boundaries were a punishment I inflicted on others rather than a form of self-care I was providing for myself.

This guilt was compounded by well-meaning but misguided advice to "forgive and forget" or *"be the bigger person."* It was as if my healing depended on extending olive branches to people still wielding chainsaws.

Dr. Harriet Lerner distinguishes between Forgiveness and boundaries in her book The Dance of Connection. She writes, "Forgiveness is not the same as reconciliation. We may forgive someone without re-establishing the relationship or reconcile without forgiving."

This distinction was revolutionary for me. I could set boundaries – even very firm ones, like no contact – without having to forgive the person I was setting boundaries with. My boundaries weren't about punishing them; they were about protecting myself. And I didn't need to forgive someone to recognise that I deserved protection.

In practical terms, this has looked like:

- Limiting contact with family members who continue to violate my boundaries
- Ending relationships with people who refuse to respect my needs and limits
- Being transparent and direct about my expectations in relationships
- Following through with consequences when boundaries are crossed

- Not justifying or over-explaining my boundaries to people who don't respect them
- Recognising that "No" is a complete sentence that doesn't require elaboration

Setting these boundaries hasn't always been easy. I've faced guilt, backlash, and accusations of being unforgiving or holding grudges. I've been told I'm "**Too sensitive**" or that I need to "**let go of the past**." I've been labelled the problem for refusing to tolerate problematic behaviour.

But I've learned that these reactions often say more about the other person's discomfort with boundaries than my right to have them. People who are used to crossing your boundaries will usually react negatively when you start enforcing them. That doesn't mean your boundaries are wrong; they're working.

Dr Nedra Glover Tawwab, a therapist and boundaries expert, emphasises that *"Boundaries are the distance at which I can love you and me simultaneously."* They're not walls that keep others out but guidelines that define how we want to be treated in relationships.

For trauma survivors, boundaries are especially important because our boundaries were often violated in the traumatic experiences themselves. Learning to set up and maintain healthy boundaries is part of reclaiming our autonomy and agency and saying, *"What happened to me before was not okay, and I get to decide how I'm treated now."*

This doesn't mean we need to cut off everyone who's ever hurt us or never give us a second chance. Based on our needs and the other person's behaviour, we get to decide what kind of relationship (if any) serves our healing and wellbeing.

Sometimes, the most healing choice is maintaining a relationship with clear, firm boundaries. Other times, the most healing choice is to end a relationship that continues to cause harm. Either way, the choice is ours based on what supports our healing, not external pressure to forgive or reconcile.

And here's the kicker: setting boundaries without requiring Forgiveness doesn't mean we're holding onto resentment or bitterness. It means we're holding onto our worth and right to be treated respectfully. It means we prioritise our healing over social expectations or others' comfort.

As the saying goes, *"You don't have to set yourself on fire to keep others warm."* Or, as we might say up North, *"You don't have to be a doormat just because someone wants to wipe their feet."*

The Healing Toolkit: Or, What to Do When You're Having a Shit Day

Even with all the healing work I've done, I still have days when trauma symptoms flare up, when triggers catch me off guard, or when life stressors push me outside my window of tolerance. The difference now is that I have a toolkit of practices and strategies that help me return to regulation rather than spiralling into prolonged distress.

I think of this toolkit as my emotional first aid kit – not a cure-all, but a collection of tools that help me manage symptoms and support my ongoing healing. Just as you might keep plasters, antiseptics, and painkillers in a physical first aid kit, this emotional first aid kit contains resources for different psychological wounds.

Here are some of the tools that have been most helpful for me:

Grounding Techniques

When I'm feeling triggered or dissociated, grounding techniques help bring me back to the present moment and into my body. These include:

- *The 5-4-3-2-1 technique: Naming five things I can see, four things I can touch, three things I can hear, two things I can smell, and one thing I can taste*
- *Feeling my feet on the floor and noticing the sensations of contact and support*
- *Holding something cold (like an ice cube) or something with a firm texture (like a rough stone)*
- *Splashing cold water on my face or running my hands under cold water*
- *Naming objects in my environment or counting backwards from 100 to 1.*

These techniques engage my senses and bring my attention to the present moment, interrupting the cycle of triggering and helping me reconnect with my surroundings. They're like throwing a bucket of cold water on a nervous system that's caught fire.

Breathwork and Movement

The breath is one of our most powerful tools for regulating the nervous system. When I'm anxious or hyper aroused, slowing and deepening my breath helps activate the parasympathetic nervous system (the "rest and digest" response). Specific breathing practices that help me include:

- *Box breathing: breathing in your nose for a count of 4, holding for 4, breathing out for 4, holding for 4, and repeating*
- *4-7-8 breathing: breathing in for a count of 4, holding for 7, and breathing out for 8*
- *Alternate nostril breathing: Closing one nostril while inhaling through the other, then switching*

Movement is also crucial for processing the energy of trauma responses, especially when I'm stuck in fight/flight activation. Simple movements like:

- *Shaking or trembling (allowing the body to discharge excess energy)*
- *Gentle stretching or yoga*
- *Walking, especially in nature*
- *Dancing or other rhythmic movement*

These physical practices help discharge the energy of trauma responses and bring me back into my body in a safe, regulated way. They're like letting steam out of a pressure cooker before it explodes.

Self-Compassion Practices

When caught in shame spirals or harsh self-criticism, self-compassion practices help me relate to myself with kindness rather than judgment. These include:

- *Placing a hand on my heart and speaking to myself with the same kindness I would offer a good friend*
- *Using self-compassion phrases like "This is a moment of suffering. Suffering is part of being human. May I be kind to myself at this moment?"*
- *Writing a letter to myself from the perspective of a wise, compassionate friend*
- *I imagine how I would respond to a loved one in the same situation and offering that same care to myself.*

These practices counter the harsh inner critic that often accompanies trauma and helps create a more supportive internal environment for healing. They're like having an internal good parent who offers comfort and understanding rather than criticism and shame.

Mindfulness and Meditation

As a Qualified Meditation Teacher, this is my absolute go-to: Mindfulness practices help me observe my thoughts, emotions, and sensations without being completely identified. This creates space between stimulus and response, between trigger and reaction. Specific practices include:

- *Brief mindfulness meditations focusing on the breath or body sensations*
- *Noting practice: Mentally labelling thoughts, emotions, and sensations as they arise ("thinking," "feeling angry," "sensing tightness")*

- ***Body scan meditation:** Systematically bringing awareness to different parts of the body*
- ***Walking meditation:** Bringing mindful awareness to the sensations of walking*

These practices help develop the observer part of me that can witness experiences without being completely swept away by them. They're like creating a stable platform to view the stormy seas of trauma responses rather than being tossed about by every wave.

Connection and Co-Regulation

When my regulation tools aren't enough, reaching out for connection with safe others can help co-regulate my nervous system. This might look like:

- *Calling a trusted friend or family member*
- *Scheduling a session with a therapist*
- *Attending a support group meeting*
- *Spending time with pets (who are often masters of being present and regulated)*
- *Engaging in community activities that provide a sense of belonging and support*

These connections provide external support for regulation when my internal resources are depleted. They're like having a backup generator when the power goes out – sometimes, we need external energy sources and support to get our systems back online.

Creative Expression

Creative practices offer a way to express and process experiences that might be difficult to put into words. These include:

- *Writing (journaling, poetry, stories)*
- *Visual art (drawing, painting, collage)*
- *Music (playing, singing, listening)*
- *Movement and dance*
- *Drama and role-play*

These creative outlets provide us with alternative pathways for processing trauma, engaging different brain parts and allowing for expression beyond our verbal language. They're like having multiple languages to express experiences that might be ineffable in our mother tongue.

Somatic Practices

Practices that work directly with the body help address the physical dimensions of trauma. These include:

- *Progressive muscle relaxation: Tensing and then releasing different muscle groups*
- *Body mapping: Drawing or noting where I feel sensations in my body*
- *Pendulation: Moving attention between areas of activation and areas of resource or neutrality in the body*
- *Titration: Working with small amounts of activation at a time to gradually build capacity*
- *Resourcing: Connecting with sensations of support, strength, or comfort in the body*

These somatic approaches acknowledge that trauma is stored in the body, not just the mind, and work directly with physical sensations and responses. They're like speaking directly to the body in its own language rather than trying to translate everything through the mind.

Having this toolkit doesn't mean I never struggle or that I can fix every trauma response with the proper technique. But it does mean I have options and resources when trauma symptoms arise. I'm not helpless in the face of triggers; I have agency and choice in how I respond to them.

Perhaps most importantly, I've learned that different tools work in various situations and at different times. There's no one-size-fits-all approach to healing, no single practice that works for every trigger or symptom. The key is having a diverse toolkit and knowing which tool is needed at any given moment.

My therapist once told me, "*Healing isn't about never falling down; it's about knowing how to get back up.*" These tools help me get back up when trauma knocks me down, return to regulation when I get dysregulated, and find my way back to myself when I get lost in trauma responses.

The Meaning Beyond Trauma: Or, Finding Purpose Without Spiritual Bypassing

One of the most challenging aspects of healing has been forming a meaning of my traumatic experiences without falling into the trap of spiritual bypassing or toxic positivity. I didn't want to minimise the impact of trauma by claiming "**everything happens for a reason**" or "**the universe only gives you what you can handle,**" although I genuinely believe those to be correct. But I also didn't want to remain stuck in a narrative of victimhood where trauma defined my entire identity and life story.

Finding a middle path between these extremes has been crucial for my healing. It involves acknowledging the full impact of trauma – the pain, loss, and damage it caused – while also recognising my capacity for growth, resilience, and meaning-making in its aftermath.

Dr. Viktor Frankl, a Holocaust survivor and psychiatrist, wrote in *"Man's Search for Meaning"* that *"suffering ceases to be suffering at the moment it finds a meaning."* This doesn't mean suffering is reasonable or necessary, but finding meaning in our experiences can transform our relationship with them.

For me, meaning-making has taken various forms:

- Using my experiences to help others through writing, speaking, and advocacy
- Developing greater compassion for myself and others who suffer
- Recognising how my trauma has shaped my values and priorities in ways that align with who I want to be
- Finding purpose in breaking generational patterns of trauma in my family
- Creating art and writing that transforms pain into beauty and connection

This meaning-making isn't about claiming that trauma was *"worth it"* or happened for some divine purpose. It's about recognising that while I didn't choose what happened to me, I can choose how I respond to it and what I create from it.

Zelda Marsh

Dr Rachel Yehuda, a leading researcher in trauma and resilience, emphasises that post-traumatic growth isn't about being grateful for trauma but about recognising the ways our responses to it have transformed us. It's not *"Thank goodness this terrible thing happened because look how much better I am now,"* but *"Despite this terrible thing that happened, I've found ways to grow and create meaning."*

This distinction is crucial because it honours the reality of trauma's impact and our capacity for growth and meaning-making. It doesn't minimise suffering or suggest that trauma is necessary for growth, but it also doesn't define us solely as victims without agency or capacity for transformation.

Finding this balance has been especially challenging in a culture that often veers toward toxic positivity – the insistence that we should always be positive, that every cloud has a silver lining, and that we should *"just be grateful"* regardless of our circumstances. This kind of forced positivity can be deeply invalidating for trauma survivors, suggesting that our pain is somehow a failure of attitude rather than a natural response to harmful experiences.

On the other hand, remaining stuck in a trauma identity without any possibility for growth or meaning can be equally limiting. If trauma is the only lens through which we view ourselves and our lives, we miss the fullness of who we are and what we're capable of beyond our wounds.

The middle path involves accepting the reality of trauma's impact and the possibility of growth and meaning-making. It's about saying, "Yes, this happened, and it was terrible, AND I am more than what happened to me. I can create meaning and purpose that honours my experiences without being defined or limited by them."

This both/and approach has been liberating for me. It allows me to acknowledge the full impact of trauma without getting stuck in victimhood. It allows me to find meaning and purpose without minimising suffering. It allows me to be both wounded and healing, scarred and whole.

As the poet Rumi wrote, "**The wound is the place where the Light enters you.**" This doesn't mean we should seek or celebrate wounds, but that if we allow them, our wounds can become doorways to deeper understanding, compassion, and connection. They can become sources of wisdom and strength rather than just sources of pain.

For me, this has meant recognising that my experiences of trauma have given me insights and capacities I might not have developed otherwise – greater empathy for others who suffer, a deeper appreciation for safety and connection, a stronger commitment to authenticity and integrity, a more nuanced understanding of the human experience.

It's also meant recognising that healing isn't just about returning to who I was before the trauma but about becoming someone new – someone who integrates both the wounds and the wisdom, both the scars and the strength, into a more whole and authentic self.

Zelda Marsh

This integration is an ongoing process, not a one-time achievement. It involves continually making and remaking meaning as I grow and change, as my understanding of my experiences evolves, and as I discover new ways of relating to my past and creating my future.

And perhaps most importantly, it involves recognising that meaning isn't something I find but something I create. It's not hidden in the trauma, waiting to be discovered like a prize in a cereal box. I actively construct it through how I choose to live in response to what has happened to me.

As Viktor Frankl wrote, *"Between stimulus and response, there is a space. In that space, we have the power to choose our response. In our response lies our growth and our freedom."* Trauma may have been the stimulus, but my response, how I heal, grow, and create meaning, is where my power and freedom lie.

The Ongoing Practice: Or, Why Healing Is a Verb, Not a Noun

The most important thing I've learned in my healing journey is that healing isn't a state we achieve once and for all but a practice we engage in day by day, moment by moment. It's not something we have, but something we do. It's a verb, not a noun.

This ongoing nature of healing can be frustrating if we're looking for a finish line, a point at which we can say, "There, I'm healed now; job done." But embracing it as a practice rather than a destination can also be liberating.

Viewing healing as a practice means:

- *We don't have to be perfectly healed to be worthy or valuable*
- *We can have bad days without it, meaning we've failed at healing*
- *We can celebrate progress without expecting perfection*
- *We can be both healing and struggling at the same time*
- *We can recognise healing as a lifelong journey rather than a finite task.*

This practice-oriented approach aligns with what psychologist Carol Dweck calls a "growth mindset", the belief that our abilities and qualities can be developed through dedication and hard work. Applied to healing, a growth mindset means believing that we can continue to heal and grow throughout our lives, that setbacks are part of the process rather than evidence of failure, and that our capacity for healing isn't fixed but can expand with practice and support.

Zelda Marsh

This has meant shifting from asking, "Am I healed yet?" to asking, "How am I practising healing today?" It means recognising that healing isn't something I achieve once and for all, but something I practice in small and large ways daily.

Some days, practising healing might look like:

- *Setting a boundary with someone who's crossing my limits*
- *Noticing when I'm triggered and using tools to return to regulation*
- *Speaking to myself with compassion rather than criticism*
- *Reaching out for support when I'm struggling*
- *Celebrating small victories and moments of joy*
- *Engaging in practices that support my well-being*
- *Choosing connection over isolation*
- *Being honest about my experiences rather than hiding or pretending*

On other days, practising healing might look more like:

- *Allowing myself to rest when I'm depleted*
- *Acknowledging when I'm struggling without shame or judgment*
- *Giving myself permission to feel difficult emotions*
- *Being gentle with myself when I fall back into old patterns*
- *Recognising that healing isn't linear and setbacks are part of the process*
- *Adjusting my expectations to match my current capacity*

- ***Remembering that I'm doing the best I can with the resources I have***

This practice-oriented approach to healing has been both challenging and liberating for me. It's challenging because there's no point at which I can say, "I'm done now; I don't have to work at this anymore." But it's liberating because it means I don't have to be perfectly healed to live a meaningful life, have valuable relationships, or pursue my goals and dreams.

It's like learning to play a musical instrument; you don't practice until you reach perfection, and then stop practising. You practice because the practice itself is valuable. After all, there's always more to learn and explore. After all, the playing itself brings joy and meaning even as you continue to develop your skills.

Similarly, we don't practice healing until we reach some perfect state of being healed and then stop. We practice healing because the practice itself is valuable, there's always more to learn and explore about ourselves, and the journey itself brings growth and meaning even as we continue to heal.

This doesn't mean we don't make progress or that healing is an endless treadmill with no tangible results. We do make progress, often significant progress. Triggers that once devastated me for days now might affect me for hours or minutes. Relationships that once seemed impossible are now sources of joy and support. Parts of myself that I once rejected or feared are now integrated and valued.

Zelda Marsh

But this progress isn't a straight line to a fixed destination; it's more like a spiral in which we revisit similar themes at deeper levels as we grow and change. The practice continues not because we're failing at healing but because healing itself is a lifelong process of growth, integration, and becoming more fully ourselves.

As the poet Mary Oliver asks, "Tell me, what do you plan to do with your one wild and precious life?" For me, practising healing is part of my answer to that question. Not because I'm broken and need to be fixed, but because healing is how I honour my experiences, reclaim my wholeness, and create a life aligned with my deepest values and most authentic self.

It's how I transform wounds into wisdom, pain into purpose, trauma into truth-telling. It's how I break generational patterns and create new possibilities for myself and others. It's how I live, not just despite what happened to me but with the fullness of who I am, including what happened to me.

Perhaps most importantly, it's how I reclaim my power from those who hurt me, not by forgetting or minimising what happened, but by refusing to let it define or limit who I am and what's possible for my life. By choosing, again and again, to practice healing rather than remaining stuck in trauma, I assert my fundamental right to wholeness, joy, and a life of my own making.

This doesn't mean I never struggle or that healing is always easy. There are still days when trauma feels overwhelming, when old patterns reassert themselves and when the path forward seems unclear or impossible. But the practice continues even on those days, perhaps especially on those days. Not perfectly, not without stumbling, but persistently, compassionately, one moment at a time.

Rumi wrote, "*As you walk on the way, the way appears.*" The practice of healing is like that we don't always know exactly where we're going or how we'll get there, but as we take each step, the next step becomes clearer. Over time, those steps add up to a journey of transformation that, while never complete, is profound and meaningful in its own right.

So, if you're reading this and wondering if you'll ever be **"fully healed,"** I invite you to consider a different question: How might your relationship with healing change if you viewed it as a practice rather than a destination? What would it mean to practice healing today, in this moment, with whatever resources and capacity you currently have?

The truth is, you don't have to be fully healed to be worthy of love, to have meaningful relationships, to pursue your goals and dreams, or to live a life aligned with your values. You can be both healing and whole, both a work in progress and complete in your fundamental humanity. The most liberating truth is that healing isn't about becoming someone different or better but about fully yourself, with all your complexities, contradictions, wounds, and wisdom. It's about reclaiming the parts of yourself that trauma disconnected you from and integrating all the parts of your experience into a more whole and authentic self.

Zelda Marsh

As Carl Jung said, "I am not what happened to me; I am what I choose to become." The practice of healing is about making that choice repeatedly, day by day, moment by moment, not perfectly, not without stumbling, but persistently, compassionately, for as long as we live.

Healing isn't something we do until we're fixed; it's a way of being in a relationship with ourselves and our experiences that honours both our wounds and our capacity for growth, our pain and our potential, who we've been and who we're becoming.

In that ongoing practice, we find not just healing but wholeness, not despite our wounds but including them, not by erasing our past but by integrating it into a present and future of our own making, not by forgetting what happened to us but by remembering who we are beyond what happened to us.

And that is the true meaning of healing, not an absence of wounds but a presence of wholeness, not a perfect state but a practice of becoming more fully ourselves, more fully human, more fully alive. Not despite what happened to us, but with the fullness of who we are, including what happened to us.

- ***In the end, healing isn't about becoming someone different but more fully yourself. And that is a practice worth engaging in for a lifetime.***

Conclusion: The Light Gets In

Well, here we are, love. We've been through the bloody wringer together, haven't we? From birth trauma to ancestral bollocks, from body memories to nervous system meltdowns, and finally to that messy, imperfect thing we call healing.

If you're waiting for the part where I tell you everything's sorted now that I float through life on a cloud of Zen-like calm, never triggered, never wobbling, you've clearly not been paying attention. That's not how this works. That's not how any of this works.

The Myth of "Completely Healed"

Let's be crystal clear about something: there's no such thing as **completely healed**." If anyone tries to sell you that particular brand of snake oil, check if they're also flogging magic beans and bridges.

Healing isn't a destination. It's not some glittering finish line where confetti falls from the sky, and a booming voice announces, *"CONGRATULATIONS! YOU'RE NO LONGER AFFECTED BY YOUR TRAUMA!"*

That's a load of absolute codswallop.

Healing is more like learning to live with a wonky knee. Some days, you hardly notice it. Other days, the weather changes, and suddenly you're hobbling about like your gran after too many sherries at Christmas. The difference is that you know why it's playing up, you've got your heat packs and exercises ready, and you don't spend hours berating your knee for being a useless, broken mess.

Just think, *"Ah, knee's playing up today,"* and adjust accordingly.

That's what healing looks like. Not a perfect adaptation.

The Body: From Enemy to Ally

For decades, I treated my body like she was the enemy. **The betrayer**. The one who kept the score when I desperately wanted to wipe the slate clean.

Every pain was an inconvenience. Every panic attack was a weakness. Every gut reaction was an overreaction.

I was at war with the very thing keeping me alive.

What a bloody waste of energy that was.

The most profound shift in my healing journey wasn't learning to forgive others; it was learning to stop fighting my own body. Recognising every symptom, trigger, and seemingly irrational response was information. Valuable information.

My body wasn't betraying me. She was protecting me; it was the only way she knew how to use the tools she'd developed in response to genuine threats.

The problem wasn't her response; it was happening in situations where it wasn't needed anymore, like a smoke alarm that goes off when you're making toast because it once detected an actual fire (true story).

The alarm isn't broken. It's doing exactly what it's designed to do. It just needs recalibration.

And that's what healing is: not silencing the alarm but recalibrating it, not ignoring your body's wisdom but learning to interpret it more accurately.

Boundaries: The Unsung Heroes of Healing

If there's one thing I wish someone had tattooed on my forehead when I was younger, it's this: **"Your boundaries are not negotiable,"** or at least shown me what boundaries were!!

For too long, I thought setting boundaries was selfish, mean, and even. Good people, kind people, should always be available to everyone, regardless of the cost to themselves.

What a crock of absolute shite.

Boundaries aren't walls. They're not about shutting people out but about letting yourself in. They're about recognising your limited energy, time, and emotional capacity and consciously choosing how to allocate those precious resources.

And here's the kicker: you don't need anyone's permission to set a boundary. You don't need to justify, explain, or apologise for it.

"*No*" is a complete sentence, love.

"*I'm uncomfortable with that*" doesn't require a follow-up explanation.

"*This doesn't work for me*" isn't an invitation for negotiation.

Learning this: really learning it, not just intellectually but in my bones, has been more healing than a thousand therapy sessions. Boundaries aren't just about what you say to others but about what you say to yourself.

They're a way of telling your nervous system, "***I've got you. I won't put you in situations that overwhelm you. I won't sacrifice your well-being for someone else's comfort.***"

And when does your nervous system finally believe you? That's when the real healing begins.

The Freedom Beyond Forgiveness

Let's reevaluate where we started this whole forgiveness malarkey.

I'm not against forgiveness as a concept. If it works for you, brings you peace, and helps you move forward, crack on, love. I'm genuinely happy for you.

But for many of us, especially those who've experienced profound betrayal, abuse, or abandonment, forgiveness can feel like another burden. Another thing we're failing at. Another way we're not "*healing properly.*"

And that's just not on.

The truth is, you can heal without forgiving, move forward without making peace with those who hurt you, and reclaim your life, joy, and sense of self without ever uttering the words, "*I forgive you.*"

What you can't do, what none of us can, is heal while holding onto the hope that those who hurt us will suddenly recognise the damage they've done, take responsibility for it, and make amends.

That's not forgiveness. That's fantasy.

Real healing happens when you stop waiting for apologies that may never come, when you stop needing the person who hurt you to acknowledge that hurt, when you recognise that your healing is not dependent on anyone else's actions, words, or recognition.

It happens when you realise that the opposite of resentment isn't forgiveness, it's indifference.

When you can think about the person who hurt you and feel… nothing much at all. No rage, pain, or burning desire for them to suffer as you have. Just a calm acknowledgement: "**That happened. It shaped me. But it doesn't define me.**"

That's freedom. And it doesn't require forgiveness to achieve.

Zelda Marsh

The Light Gets In

There's a Leonard Cohen lyric I've always loved: ***"There is a crack in everything. That's how the light gets in."***

For years, I thought my trauma had broken me beyond repair. I walked around with these great, gaping cracks everyone could see. That I was fundamentally damaged in ways that "**normal**" people weren't.

I've come to understand that I shone the brightest in those cracks where I've been broken and put back together.

Through those cracks, empathy flows, deep connection happens, and authentic healing for myself and others becomes possible.

I'm not healed despite my trauma. I'm healed through it.

And so are you.

Every time, you choose to stay present instead of dissociating. Every time, you set a boundary instead of abandoning yourself. Every time you listen to your body instead of fighting it. Every time you speak your truth instead of swallowing it.

That's healing. That's light getting in through the cracks.

And it doesn't require anyone's forgiveness but your own.

A FINAL WORD (OR SEVERAL, BECAUSE I'M NORTHERN, AND WE DON'T DO BREVITY)

If you take nothing else from this book, take this: **your healing belongs to you. Not to the people who hurt you. Not to the therapists, gurus, or well-meaning friends who tell you how you "should" be doing it. Not even to me and my Northern ramblings.*

*Your healing is as unique as your trauma. There is no one-size-fits-all approach, perfect timeline, or checklist to complete before you can call yourself "**healed**."*

There is only the messy, non-linear, sometimes hilarious, sometimes heartbreaking journey of reclaiming yourself, of making peace not with those who hurt you but with the broken parts of yourself.

And on that journey, you'll find that forgiveness is not the goal but a possible by-product, if it comes at all. Something that might happen naturally once you've done the real work of healing.

Or it might not. And that's okay, too.

Zelda Marsh

Because you don't need forgiveness to heal.

You need you.

The real you: messy, complex, resilient, magnificent you, who has survived everything life has thrown at you and is still here, reading and reaching for something better.

That's enough. You're enough.

And don't let anyone, including that critical voice in your head, tell you otherwise.

Now go put the kettle on. You've earned a brew after all this emotionally heavy lifting.

And so, have I.

Final Reflection Prompt: What parts of your healing journey have been most surprising to you? What cracks in your own life have unexpectedly let the light in? Please take a moment to acknowledge how far you've come, not despite your trauma, but through it.

Epilogue

Zelda Marsh

WHERE I AM NOW (AND HOW THE BLOODY HELL I GOT HERE)

So, you've stuck with me through twelve chapters of trauma, tears, and terrible jokes. Congratulations: you're either a glutton for punishment or found something in these pages that resonates. Either way, I'm glad you're still here.

You might be wondering what happened after all the healing revelations, after the boundaries were set, after I stopped chasing forgiveness like it was the last bus home on a Saturday night.

Well, I'm still here, aren't I? Still, Northern is sarcastic and swearing like a docker with a stubbed toe. Some things never change, thank God. But other things? They've changed beyond recognition.

The Daily Practice of Being Human

> I'd love to tell you that I wake up every morning, do two hours of yoga, journal while sipping organic green tea, and float through my day in a bubble of perfect nervous system regulation.

But that would be absolute bollocks, wouldn't it?

The truth is messier, more human, and infinitely more interesting.

Some days, I still wake up with that familiar knot of anxiety. Some days, old triggers still catch me off guard. Some days, I still find myself slipping into people-pleasing patterns before I catch myself.

The difference is that now I notice. I don't beat myself up about it. I don't see it as evidence that I'm "failing" at healing or that all my work has been for nothing.

I think, *"Oh, hello, old pattern. I see you there."* Then, I consciously choose whether to follow that pattern or try something different.

That's what healing looks like in real life: not perfection, but awareness. It is not the absence of triggers but the presence of choice in how you respond to them.

The Ripple Effect

One of the most unexpected outcomes of my healing journey has been its impact on others. Not because I've gone around preaching the gospel of trauma recovery (God forbid), but because healing changes how you move through the world. And people notice.

They notice when you stop abandoning yourself to please others. They notice when you speak your truth instead of swallowing it. They notice when you set boundaries instead of building resentments. And some of those who are ready will be inspired to do the same.

I've watched friends start their own healing journeys, family members begin to question generational patterns, and colleagues start setting boundaries they never thought they deserved.

Not because I told them to, but because they saw it was possible. They saw that you could heal without forgiveness, that you could break cycles without breaking yourself, and that you could honour your trauma without being defined by it.

That's how change happens, not through grand gestures or perfect examples, but through ordinary people doing the extraordinary work of reclaiming themselves, one day at a time.

The Book You're Holding

Writing this book has been a healing journey. There were days when the words flowed like I'd turned on a tap, and days when extracting a single sentence felt like pulling teeth with a pair of rusty pliers.

There were moments when I thought, "**Who am I to write this? Who's going to listen to me?**" The old impostor syndrome is alive and well despite years of healing work.

But then I'd remember all the books I'd read on trauma and healing, the clinical ones that made me feel like a case study rather than a person, the spiritual ones that made me feel like I wasn't "transcending" my trauma properly, the self-help ones that reduced complex neurobiological processes to five easy steps and a positive affirmation.

And I'd think, "*That's why I need to write this. Because someone out there needs to hear it this way, unfiltered, sometimes funny, deeply human.*"

Someone must know they're not alone in finding the forgiveness narrative toxic. Someone needs to know they're not failing at healing just because they still get triggered sometimes. Someone needs to know that their body isn't the enemy: it's been their ally all along, doing its best with the information it had.

If that someone is you, then every late night, every tear shed, every moment of vulnerability it took to write these words has been worth it.

Zelda Marsh

WHAT COMES NEXT

People often ask me, "**What's next on your healing journey**?" as if there's some final destination I haven't reached yet.

But that's not how I think about it anymore. Healing isn't a journey with a destination; it's more like tending a garden. Some seasons are about growth, others about rest. Sometimes, you're planting new seeds; other times, you're pulling weeds that have crept back in.

The work is never "done," but that doesn't mean you're doing it wrong. It just means you're alive, constantly evolving, and continually responding to new challenges and opportunities for growth.

So what's next for me? I will live with as much presence and authenticity as I can muster on any given day. I will continue to listen to my body instead of fighting it, set boundaries instead of building resentments, and choose connection over protection when it's safe.

> I will continue to share my story: not because it's extraordinary, but precisely because it isn't. **Trauma is ordinary. Healing is ordinary.** And finding our way back to ourselves is the most ordinary and sacred journey of all.

Following and complementing this book, there will be a "I Don't Need Your Forgiveness to Heal" journal, plus I will have a 12-week Transformational course, titled: **The Body Remember, The Soul Heals**, available on my website, www.mainfestmerriment.com

A FINAL THANK YOU

Before I go, thank you for coming on this journey with me, for reading these words, for witnessing my story, and for perhaps recognising pieces of your own story reflected back at you.

A special connection happens when one person says, "This happened to me," and another responds, "Me too." Some of the deepest healing happens in that connection, that moment of being truly seen and understood.

So, thank you for seeing me.

Know that, in whatever way you're healing, whatever path you're on, whether forgiveness is part of your journey or not, *I see you too*.

You're doing brilliantly, love. Even on the days when it doesn't feel like it. Especially on the days when it doesn't feel like it.

Keep going. The light's already getting in.

With gratitude, love and solidarity,

Zelda

Zelda Marsh

About The Author

Zelda Marsh is a trauma survivor turned truth-teller, soul-stirrer, and unapologetic voice for those who've been silenced too bloody long.

With a sharp Lincolnshire wit that could cut through steel, deep-rooted empathy that sees right through your walls, and an uncanny ability to feel what others carry, even when they can't name it themselves, she brings a fierce, heart-led approach to healing that's about as subtle as a Grimsby trawlerman after a night at the pub.

Zelda doesn't write from some fancy therapist's chair with certificates on the wall.

She writes from rock bottom. From survival. From knowing what it's like when your tea's gone cold, but you drink it anyway because you can't afford another.

From a teenage life fuelled by nicked chip shop scraps and pure Northern grit in Grimsby, and from the proper impressive rise that came after, like the tide at Cleethorpes when you've not been paying attention.

Now known as the go-to for grounded, no-nonsense healing without the airy-fairy rubbish, she helps others reconnect with their truth, regulate their nervous systems, and release pain stored in both body and spirit. As a holistic therapist qualified in NLP life coaching (both NLP and spiritual life coaching), Zelda brings professional expertise alongside lived experience that's as real as Grimsby on a rainy Tuesday. She is also the published author of "Bouncebackability: Reclaim Your Power and Passion After Divorce."

Passionate about justice, being treated properly, and doing whatever it takes to live a healthy, happy, healing life on her own terms, Zelda left England to create a new, toxic-free life in Australia. Though she's swapped the grey skies and fish docks of Grimsby for Australian sunshine and beaches, her Northern roots remain strong as a good Yorkshire brew in her no-nonsense approach to healing. Her authenticity, loving nature, and honesty shine through in everything she does, and she wishes wellness onto anyone who comes into her world, even the right prats who probably don't deserve it.

Her words are soaked in energy, truth, and intention, crafted for anyone ready to remember:

Living as your true self isn't just healing. It's powerful. It's freedom. And it's your birthright, darling.

When not writing or helping others heal, Zelda can be found, when not working enjoying a proper brew (because some British habits never die, even in 40-degree heat), reminiscing about Grimsby's fishing heritage to bewildered Australians, and occasionally shocking the locals with her colourful Lincolnshire expressions that would make a sailor blush. She still can't bring herself to call flip-flops "thongs," and firmly believes that gravy and mushy peas should be available in all restaurants, regardless of cuisine type.

References

Academic

Badenoch, B. (2018). The Heart of Trauma: Healing the Embodied Brain in the Context of Relationships. W. W. Norton & Company.

Dana, D. (2018). The Polyvagal Theory in Therapy: Engaging the Rhythm of Regulation. W. W. Norton & Company.

Fisher, J. (2017). Healing the Fragmented Selves of Trauma Survivors: Overcoming Internal Self-Alienation. Routledge.

Herman, J. L. (2015). Trauma and Recovery: The Aftermath of Violence—From Domestic Abuse to Political Terror. Basic Books.

Levine, P. A. (2015). Trauma and Memory: Brain and Body in a Search for the Living Past. North Atlantic Books.

Levine, P. A. (2010). In an Unspoken Voice: How the Body Releases Trauma and Restores Goodness. North Atlantic Books.

Maté, G. (2011). When the Body Says No: Exploring the Stress-Disease Connection. John Wiley & Sons.

Ogden, P., Minton, K., & Pain, C. (2006). Trauma and the Body: A Sensorimotor

Approach to Psychotherapy. W. W. Norton & Company. Can mindfulness improve health and slow ageing? | Semel Institute for Neuroscience and Human Behaviour.

Exploring the Intriguing World of Twins: A Psychological Perspective - TwinsMag. https://twinsmag.com/twins-psychology-studies/

Mental Health Experts Warn About Impacts New Regulations Could Have On Migrant Children | KERA News. https://www.keranews.org/2019-08-22/mental-health-experts-warn-about-impacts-new-regulations-could-have-on-migrant-children

Research confirms that 22.5% of Americans have a sevenfold risk of suicide. Here's why... - Health Secret. https://healthsecret.com/how-a-comprehensive-detox-helps-your-mental-health/

Marsh, Z. (2025). I DON'T NEED YOUR FORGIVENESS TO HEAL. Zelda Marsh.

432Hz |. https://www.kingblvdandwallst.com/tag/432hz/

Individual Therapy | KM Therapy | Washington State. https://km-therapy.com/individual-therapy/

How To Make Your Hair Grow Faster And Stronger | Raw Hair Shop. https://skyhairvn.com/how-to-make-your-hair-grow-faster-and-stronger/https://www.semel.ucla.edu/longevity/news/can-mindfulness-improve-health-and-slow-aging

Porges, S. W. (2011). The Polyvagal Theory: Neurophysiological Foundations of Emotions, Attachment, Communication, and Self-regulation. W. W. Norton & Company.

Rothschild, B. (2000). The Body Remembers: The Psychophysiology of Trauma and Trauma Treatment. W. W. Norton & Company.

Scaer, R. (2014). The Body Bears the Burden: Trauma, Dissociation, and Disease. Routledge.

Schwartz, R. C. (2001). Introduction to the Internal Family Systems Model. Trailheads Publications.

Siegel, D. J. (2012). **The Developing Mind:** How Relationships and the Brain Interact to Shape Who We Are. Guilford Press.

van der Kolk, B. (2014). The Body Keeps the Score: Brain, Mind, and Body in the Healing of Trauma. Viking.

Walker, P. (2013). Complex PTSD: From Surviving to Thriving: A Guide and Map for Recovering from Childhood Trauma. Azure Coyote.

Wolynn, M. (2016). It Didn't Start with You: How Inherited Family Trauma Shapes Who We Are and How to End the Cycle. Viking.

Yehuda, R., & Bierer, L. M. (2009). The relevance of epigenetics to PTSD: Implications for the DSM-V. Journal of Traumatic Stress, 22(5), 427-434.

ADDITIONAL RESOURCES

Books

Brach, T. (2013). True Refuge: Finding Peace and Freedom in Your Own Awakened Heart. Bantam.

Brown, B. (2015). Rising Strong: How the Ability to Reset Transforms the Way We Live, Love, Parent, and Lead. Random House.

Heller, L., & LaPierre, A. (2012). **Healing Developmental Trauma:** How Early Trauma Affects

Self-Regulation, Self-Image, and the Capacity for Relationship. North Atlantic Books.

Karr-Morse, R., & Wiley, M. S. (2012). Scared Sick: The Role of Childhood Trauma in Adult Disease. Basic Books.

Kolk, B. van der. (2014). The Body Keeps the Score: Brain, Mind, and Body in the Healing of Trauma. Viking.

Levine, P. A. (1997). Waking the Tiger: Healing Trauma. North Atlantic Books.

Maté, G. (2008). In the Realm of Hungry Ghosts: Close Encounters with Addiction. Knopf Canada.

Menakem, R. (2017). My Grandmother's Hands: Racialized Trauma and the Pathway to Mending Our Hearts and Bodies. Central Recovery Press.

Nagoski, E., & Nagoski, A. (2019). Burnout: The Secret to Unlocking the Stress Cycle. Ballantine Books.

Neff, K. (2011). Self-Compassion: The Proven Power of Being Kind to Yourself. William Morrow.

Patel, R. (2019). Wintering: The Power of Rest and Retreat in Difficult Times. Riverhead Books.

Perel, E. (2017). The State of Affairs: Rethinking Infidelity. Harper.

Tippett, K. (2016). Becoming Wise: An Inquiry into the Mystery and Art of Living. Penguin Press.

Articles and Research Papers

Anda, R. F., Felitti, V. J., Bremner, J. D., Walker, J. D., Whitfield, C., Perry, B. D., ... & Giles, W. H. (2006). The enduring effects of abuse and related adverse experiences in childhood. European Archives of Psychiatry and Clinical Neuroscience, 256(3), 174-186.

Felitti, V. J., Anda, R. F., Nordenberg, D., Williamson, D. F., Spitz, A. M., Edwards, V., ... & Marks, J. S. (1998). Relationship of childhood abuse and household dysfunction to many of the leading causes of death in adults: The Adverse Childhood Experiences (ACE) Study. American Journal of Preventive Medicine, 14(4), 245-258.

Geller, S. M., & Porges, S. W. (2014). Therapeutic presence: Neurophysiological mechanisms mediating feeling safe in therapeutic relationships. Journal of Psychotherapy Integration, 24(3), 178-192.

Porges, S. W. (2007). The polyvagal perspective. Biological Psychology, 74(2), 116-143.

Schore, A. N. (2001). The effects of early relational trauma on proper brain development, affect regulation, and infant mental health. Infant Mental Health Journal, 22(1-2), 201-269.

Teicher, M. H., & Samson, J. A. (2016). Annual research review: Enduring neurobiological effects of childhood abuse and neglect. Journal of Child Psychology and Psychiatry, 57(3), 241-266.

Yehuda, R., Daskalakis, N. P., Bierer, L. M., Bader, H. N., Klengel, T., Holsboer, F., & Binder, E. B. (2016). Holocaust exposure induced intergenerational effects on FKBP5 methylation. Biological Psychiatry, 80(5), 372-380.

Online Resources

The National Child Traumatic Stress Network: www.nctsn.org

The Trauma Research Foundation: www.traumaresearchfoundation.org

The Polyvagal Institute: www.polyvagalinstitute.org

The Centre for Mind-Body Medicine: www.cmbm.org

The Somatic Experiencing Trauma Institute: www.traumahealing.org

The International Society for Traumatic Stress Studies: www.istss.org

The Adverse Childhood Experiences (ACE) Study: www.cdc.gov/violenceprevention/aces

Podcasts and Audio Resources

"The Body Keeps the Score" with Dr. Bessel van der Kolk (On Being with Krista Tippett)

"Healing Trauma and Spiritual Growth" with Dr. Gabor Maté (Sounds True)

"Unlocking Us" with Brené Brown (Episodes on trauma and resilience)

"The Trauma Therapist Podcast" with Guy Macpherson

"The Polyvagal Podcast" with Deb Dana

"Where Should We Begin?" with Esther Perel

"Therapy Chat" with Laura Reagan

Apps and Digital Tools

Insight Timer (Guided meditations for trauma recovery)

Calm Harm (For managing urges to self-harm)¡

Zelda Marsh

Headspace (Mindfulness and meditation)

Calm (Sleep stories and meditation)

Waking Up (Mindfulness and meditation with Sam Harris)å

Liberate (Meditation for the Black, Indigenous, and People of Colour community)

Somatic Practices and Movement Therapies

Trauma-Sensitive Yoga (David Emerson and Bessel van der Kolk)

Somatic Experiencing (Peter Levine)

Sensorimotor Psychotherapy (Pat Ogden)

TRE (Tension and Trauma Releasing Exercises) (David Berceli)

EMDR (Eye Movement Desensitisation and Reprocessing) (Francine Shapiro)

Hakomi Method (Ron Kurtz)

Feldenkrais Method (Moshe Feldenkrais)

Alexander Technique (F. Matthias Alexander)

Authentic Movement (Mary Starks Whitehouse)

5Rhythms (Gabrielle Roth)

Community Support Resources

Adult Children of Alcoholics and Dysfunctional Families (ACA): www.adultchildren.org

Survivors Network: www.snapnetwork.org

RAINN (Rape, Abuse & Incest National Network): www.rainn.org

National Domestic Violence Hotline: www.thehotline.org

Survivors of Incest Anonymous: www.siawso.org

Co-Dependents Anonymous: www.coda.org

Al-Anon Family Groups: www.al-anon.org

Trauma Recovery Groups: www.traumarecoverygroups.org

www.ingramcontent.com/pod-product-compliance
Lightning Source LLC
Chambersburg PA
CBHW071234070526
44583CB00017B/2182